Playing to Learn

Sandra Smidt sets out to explain what play is and why it is so important as one of the key ways of learning, particularly – but not solely – for young children. She argues that *all* play is purposeful and can only truly considered to be play when the child has chosen what to do, where and how to do it.

Using case studies drawn from all over the world, Smidt challenges some of the prevailing myths relating to play and pays close attention to what early years professionals need to do to interpret the play, understand its purpose for the child and sometimes extend it.

Attention is paid to the close links that play has with creativity, and the author also highlights the importance of being able to explain to colleagues, parents and even those in government, why play matters so much in terms of learning and development.

This book will be of interest to anyone involved in early years education.

Sandra Smidt is a retired educationalist, who now writes on aspects of early learning and development. Her most recent books include: *Key Issues in Early Years Education; Introducing Vygotsky; Supporting Multilingual Learners in the Early Years* and *A Guide to Early Years Education, 3rd edition*, all published by Routledge.

Playing to Learn

The role of play in the early years

Sandra Smidt

Routledge
Taylor & Francis Group

LONDON AND NEW YORK

This edition published 2011
by Routledge
2 Park Square, Milton Park, Abingdon, Oxon OX14 4RN

Simultaneously published in the USA and Canada
by Routledge
711 Third Avenue, New York, NY 10017 (8th Floor)

Routledge is an imprint of the Taylor & Francis Group,
an informa business

Typeset in Optima by Glyph International

British Library Cataloguing in Publication Data
A catalogue record for this book is available from the British Library

Library of Congress Cataloging-in-Publication Data
Smidt, Sandra, 1943-
Playing to learn : the role of play in the early years/Sandra Smidt.
    p. cm.
Includes bibliographical references and index.
1. Play. 2. Learning. 3. Child development. I. Title.
LB1137.S585 2010
155.4'18--dc22   2009046047

ISBN 13: 978-0-415-55881-5 (hbk)
ISBN 13: 978-0-415-55882-2 (pbk)
ISBN 13: 978-0-203-85199-9 (ebk)

For all the serious and joyful and questioning players wherever they are and for those who take their play seriously

Contents

Introduction

This is a book about play, but it needs to be emphasised that it is not a book advocating what might be described as a traditional play-based curriculum. Rather, it is a book which looks to examine why play is such a powerful way of learning for many children and which seeks to critique the now-accepted play/work dichotomy. In order to do this, play is re-defined, insisting that it is always purposeful for the players and rarely trivial. Play is seen as serious, sometimes difficult, sometimes pleasurable, usually satisfying for the player and closely related to creativity. There is a strong argument for a pedagogy that is based on mutual respect, attentive listening, sensitive intervention and strong relationships. Such a pedagogy does not require expensive or specialist equipment or resourcing, and draws on the experiences each child brings to the setting. The book seeks to offer a way of thinking about play which takes account of different styles of learning, of living and of developing for children coming from a range of family structures. Where possible, research from across the world is drawn on, although examples from the developing world are hard to find and there is some evident feeling that play (as described in much of the writing) presents an idealised view of childhood that is extremely at odds with the reality of the lives of the majority of the world's children.

The book starts with a chapter defining play and introducing some of the ideas of theorists, researchers and others into the field of play and learning. Sadly many (but not all) of these are based in the developed world and refer to Western society, many seeing play as preparation for what we might call 'real' life. Some manage to go beyond an idealised view of childhood and play and offer insights that seem to be wider and more globally applicable: Vygotsky, Bruner, Trevarthen and Rogoff in particular, and more recent people such as Moyles, Goouch and Roopnarine.

The examples and vignettes are drawn from a range of sources – from books, from personal observation, from examples offered by colleagues and students – and they reflect the experiences of children in many countries, from different cultures and communities, with different languages and customs. Embedded in most of the chapters is a case study. The first of these refers to early pioneers in the field of play. All the others are drawn from the developing and the developed worlds to illustrate similarities and differences in thinking and practice, issues and solutions, philosophy and funding.

I am grateful to all those who submitted observation notes, comments, opinions, samples of children's work and anecdotes about children at play. I am delighted to have been offered drawings and bits of writing by some of my grandchildren and the grandchildren of some of my friends. I enjoyed many conversations and some almost arguments with colleagues and friends whose passions and feelings ran high on a subject dear to all our hearts. And yet again I owe a debt of gratitude to my friend Hazel Abel who agreed to read through the second draft to offer her views.

Note: Throughout the book 'she' is used rather than the more accepted and common 'he'.

Chapter 1

What is this thing called play?

The book starts by defining play and then moves on to introducing the ideas of some of the people whose thinking and writing have been influential on educators, researchers and writers. Here you encounter some of the professional language or 'jargon' associated with the subject. Each such term or phrase is given in italic script and explained in the text that follows. This means that by the end of this chapter you should have a framework on which to build a more complex and nuanced understanding of what is meant by play and of why play matters.

> 'We don't stop playing because we grow old; we grow old because we stop playing.'
>
> (George Bernard Shaw)

> 'You can discover more about a person in an hour of play than in a year of conversation.'
>
> (Plato)

NOTES:

 Since this book has been written with teachers, nursery nurses, teaching assistants, those working in Children's Centres and other educators and practitioners in mind, the implications of what is said for these professionals is key. In order to make such implications evident, this logo is used. You might find it at the head of a whole section or dotted in the midst of the text.

The voices of practitioners are highlighted in the text where they comment directly on their own views and practice. This logo makes this clear to readers.

Starting with a definition

> Play is what children and young people do when they follow their own ideas and their own interests in their own way for their own reasons.
> (Getting Serious About Play – DCMS, 2004)

It seems odd, in 2009, to be writing yet another book about play. So much has been thought and said and argued and written about it that it seems impossible to believe that there is more to say. You can read countless definitions of play and find it referred to in government documents and text books on early learning. And yet play still seems to be a misunderstand concept and the term is used so loosely that perhaps another book is truly needed.

Play can be defined as the way in which children within a context, a culture, a family and a community, set about doing any or all of the following:

- trying to solve a problem they have set themselves;
- exploring and experiencing something that interests or concerns or scares or excites them;
- expressing and communicating their feelings related to their experiences.

Play is thus always purposeful for the child.

You can quickly see in this definition the sense of *agency*: it is the child who needs to solve a problem or experience or express or explore something. No one needs to tell the child to do these things. From this it follows that *all play is purposeful* because the child is using it for a reason. The child owns the reason and therefore the play. The child is in control of what to do and how to do it. The play itself may well be pleasurable or fun, but it may also be deeply disturbing and traumatic. So play is what the learner chooses to do in order to address a need, answer a question, express a feeling or follow up an interest.

This definition might raise some questions – for example, what is meant by talking of play as 'traumatic' or what is meant by adult-directed play or where is the role of the practitioner in play where the child is in control of the agenda. These are important and valid questions which will be addressed throughout the book. By the end of the book you may have been persuaded that we should only describe behaviour as play where it is purposeful: purposeful does not necessarily mean consciously purposeful.

Key thinkers in the field

Note: Many important ideas and issues will be raised in this introductory chapters. All the ideas raised here will be dealt with in more detail in the chapters that follow. Remember that this is a scene-setting chapter, designed as an introduction to some complex ideas and language. The key thinkers are not introduced in chronological order; rather they are introduced in a sequence reflecting their particular views on play and how they relate to the arguments of this book.

Many writers, thinkers and researchers have discussed play and its importance in learning. We start with the ideas of Jerome Bruner who was very interested in play as a way or a *mode of learning* which implies that he saw it not as an activity in itself but as a way of doing something. We can do things because we have been asked or told to do them, or because we feel the need to do them. For example, the child can fill containers in the water tray because she has been told to or because she has chosen to. In the first example the child may be learning through following an instruction; in the second, she is learning through play because she is seeking an answer to a question she has raised.

The child engaged in play is finding out about the world and the objects and people and relationships in it. Bruner saw *play is a process*. We know that there are many modes or ways of learning – for example, reading or watching an 'expert' or exploring or asking questions. Bruner's position was to see play as another way of learning. Famously he talked of play as *'memory in action'* and this is something worth spending some time considering. What Bruner meant by this was that children play in order to remember and think about events and experiences in their lives that are no longer present and in order to make sense of them. The example of a child dropping things one after another out of the pram is not an example of random behaviour but rather suggests that the child is implicitly asking a question – perhaps 'Why do these things land on the ground? Do all things do this? What would happen if I threw it up in the air first?' and so on. Describing play as memory in action is a powerful way of allowing practitioners and others to think differently about play and about its significance. Bruner's focus on the links between play and memory allows us to see play as always purposeful for the child.

Play is a way of being able to use *hands-on* or *real* or *life-like situations* to answer questions that arise in children's heads as they constantly seek to make sense of their lives, experiences and feelings. Very young children, when encountering something new, appear to *ask* themselves 'What is this?' and then to attempt to answer the question by using what is available to them. Their asking of a question is not, of course, using words, but their behaviour is indicative of a search for meaning. And in the earliest years the ways in which they can seek to make sense of anything are all very concrete. They can touch and mouth and look at and listen to and shake or drop or feel or smell whatever it is. As they do this, it seems likely that they then *compare* whatever it is they are exploring with other things they have explored. This is where memory comes in. So in the earliest months of life, children use movement and their senses to explore new objects or experiences or people and to compare them with other things they have encountered. At this stage children do not yet have access to words to describe these comparisons. Access to spoken language comes through their interactions with others in their lives and is one of the most important *cultural tools* to help learning. (The term 'cultural tools' was first used by Vygotsky to describe things that have been made by human beings in order to assist their thinking and communication. Examples of cultural tools include complex systems like language, books, signs, symbols and artefacts. You will find more about cultural tools and their significance throughout the book.)

As children get older, their store of experiences becomes greater so they have more memory to rely on. Let's look at some examples to illustrate this:

- Three-month-old Nuur, given a shiny rattle, puts it in her mouth, takes it out, looks at it, shakes it accidentally and hears the sound it makes, puts it back in her mouth, takes it out again, looks at it and shakes it again more purposefully. Two days later, given the same rattle, she immediately shakes it, listens, smiles, shakes it again.
- Fifteen-month-old Dov is given a doll when his new brother is born. He holds the doll, rocks it in his arms, looks into its face and smiles, rocks it again and then puts it in a pram. Six weeks later he only ever takes the doll out of its pram in order to throw in on the floor and stamp on it.
- Lerato is a child being raised by his grandmother since his mother died a year ago. He finds it difficult to separate from her in the mornings when he goes to school and at school is involved in a lot of fighting. But when he comes home his grandmother says that he will listen to her tell stories about his mother and will listen for a long time and with intense concentration.
- Five-year-old Emilia has just started school. She comes home after a few days and sets her dolls out on the floor in a circle and then sings with them the songs she is learning at school.

These are simple observations, relatively easy to analyse in terms of memory in action. Let us do this.

- Nuur has very little memory to draw on when she first encounters the rattle and her initial explorations use her senses and her actions. But it is clear that she is *cognitively active*, which means that she is thinking about and noticing what happens. So that when she is next presented with the rattle, she can draw on her memory that it made a noise when she shook it. We can assume that the noise surprised or pleased or interested her which is why she tried to elicit it again.

- Dov has seen his mother rocking the new baby in her arms. Dov, being older than Nuur, has more experiences to draw on and initially he calls up the image of his mother rocking the baby and does this to the doll. A little later his play changes and he now draws on the memory he has of his *feelings* about the new baby and enacts these out using the doll. Feelings are really important to all learning and evident in much play. He solves the problem of his feelings safely through the doll rather than through his baby sister!
- Lerato's memory in action is reflected in his ability to pay attention to stories being told about his mother who tragically died when he was 4 years old. In his time at school his play is characterised by aggression, possibly showing more about his feelings than he is able to show in other ways.
- Emilia plays the role of teacher at circle time, arranging her dolls as her peers and singing the songs she has learned. This is clearly memory in action.

We now turn to the work of Tina Bruce, an educationalist whose work you may have read. She has written much about play and clearly regards it as one of the most significant ways in which young children learn. You can see the influence of the work of Bruner on her. She talks of play being '*an integrating mechanism*' and it is worth taking a little time to understand what she means by this. She says that when children are involved in what she calls '*free-flow play*' (play which is self-chosen and where they are in control of what they are doing), they appear to *bring together many aspects of their learning and coordinate them in order to bring about or reinforce new learning*. Here again it is the process which is important. The end-product, if there is one, may not be relevant to the learning that takes place. Here is an example, taken directly from Bruce (1991):

> … Anne (five years) is playing 'schools' in the garden. There is a clump of snapdragons. She pretends these are the children in the class and that she is the teacher. She pretends that it is lunchtime and tips water into each one, pulling the flowerhead apart to do so. She chats in teacher tones, 'Good boy – what a nice clean plate', etc.
>
> (p. 79)

In Bruce's analysis of this as an example of play as an integrating mechanism, she says that Anne brings together the memory of two real experiences – one of starting school and the other of having lunch with a friend whose mother is very keen on clean plates at the end of the meal. Again, the link to

Bruner's work, here to play as memory in action, is evident. We need to think about the implications of this for us. Remember that Bruner can only know this by finding out as much as possible about each child and by observing the children as they play.

 This is the first explicit reference to what practitioners need to know or do in order to understand play and use it to good effect. Practitioners need to know as much as possible about their children so that they can then watch children, listen to them and think about what their actions might indicate about their interests and their concerns.

In order to try to analyse the next example in terms of play as an integrating mechanism you need to know some things about the child involved, Diya. Bruce tells us that Diya has heard of orphanages in Romania through the children's news programmes on television and she has seen the film 'Oliver'.

> Diya (five years) plays 'orphanages' with her dolls and soft toys. She dresses them all, and sits them round a pretend table. She rings a bell – 'Don't ask for more, 'cos you won't get it' she says sternly to the teddy. She 'walks' some of the dolls round, clearing and wiping the table. She makes them all line up, blows a whistle and sends them to school.
>
> (p. 79)

No one would be able to attempt an explanation of Diya's behaviour without some knowledge about her and her experience. But equipped with some knowledge about her prior experience, it is possible for her to draw on the things she remembers and perhaps doesn't quite understand and uses them in her play to try and enhance what she currently thinks.

Sometimes when we observe children at play what we see seems to us to be random, haphazard and totally lacking in any purpose we can work out. Here are some examples:

- Zoli drew a picture, using many colours and making lines and closed shapes all over the page. She then looked closely at her picture, picked up a black felt pen and carefully covered up all the marks she had made.
- Meeny (a nickname given to him by an older brother) ran around the yard in circles. Later he was seen rotating his arms like the sails of a windmill. He scratched with a stick in the dirt, making circles big and small.
- Daisy wanted to help her mum put the clean washing away. She took her toy pram and filled it up with all the clean socks and knickers,

wheeled those into her brother's room, unpacked them onto his bed, went back to the pile of laundry and this time loaded the pram with T-shirts which she transported to the bathroom and placed in the (luckily) empty bath. She then returned to the clean socks and knickers, put them into the pram and this time wheeled them into the kitchen. And on and on.

Those of you who have heard of or read about schemas will recognise that this type of behaviour as 'schematic'. The term *schema* was first used by Jean Piaget, one of the founding fathers of psychology and someone whose work has been extremely influential on education in this country. For Piaget schemas were 'patterns of repeatable actions that lead to early categories and then to logical classifications' (Athey, 1990, p. 36). The actions include things like banging and sucking and grasping and moving and shaking objects, for example, and this results in infants discovering groups of objects that are graspable, suckable, bangable and so on.

Returning to our examples, we can see that Zoli used the physical movement of covering her drawing with thick black felt pen lines. It is possible that she was wondering something like 'Will the drawing still be there when I hide it under a thick black layer?' So her mental or cognitive actions would involve things like raising a question (will my picture still be there?) or drawing on past experience (when I pull my blanket over my head I am still where I was). Can you see the link with play as memory in action?

Piaget's focus was on the physical exploration of objects leading to classification and then to logical thinking. But later theorists believe that the physical exploration might only involve looking. The first time the child sees a dog she might notice that the creature has a furry body, several legs and is quite small. If she then sees another small dog, she might notice that it also has several legs and a furry body. She is able to form her own group or category or schema: dog = small furry creature with several legs. But if she then sees a large dog, she will still see the furry body and the legs but will have to change or *modify her previous schema*. According to Piaget her original schema of dog = small furry thing with several legs might have to be adapted to dog = furry thing with several legs. Being able to identify what features things have in common is known as *categorising* and is an important function of learning. This might help to understand Meeny's seemingly haphazard behaviour. Meeny is clearly interested in things that go round or rotate. His schema is called 'rotation' and he explores it as often as he needs to in order to understand something that interests him about his world. Perhaps he wants to know how wheels go round and round or if he can turn round and round or if his stick can make round marks in the sand.

Daisy's schema is known as 'transporting'. She is interested in using something to carry other things from one place to another. Perhaps she is asking 'Can I fit all these things into my pram?' or 'If I take things from one place to another will they still be there when I come back?' or 'What will make this pram full?' Piaget's ideas are quite difficult to understand because he used complex language to discuss them. You may have come across some of his terms, like 'assimilation' and 'accommodation'. Quite simply *assimilation* means taking something new into an existing schema. What we take in does not change our previous thinking. A young child who encounters a small dog will not have to change her category of dog = small furry creature with legs. *Accommodation* means changing our existing schema in response to something new. The child who encounters a large dog has to change her category to take account of something new that challenges this previous category. It is what Vygotsky called a *higher level of thinking* and learning and may result in refined or new schemas developing.

The implication for practitioners is that play which sometimes appears purposeless to us, is not. Even the sometimes irritating behaviours observed as children pursue their own schemas are deeply rooted in the need to make sense of the world. In effect the schemas are problem-solving behaviours.

Janet Moyles is someone else who has spent a lifetime thinking about play as a mode of learning. Her concern has been to ensure that not only children in the early years have access to learning through play, but that older children and adults can also follow their own interests and have their attempts valued and taken seriously. One of the things she regards as most significant about play is the aspect of *'ownership'*. This term might make you feel uncomfortable, thinking of it as being linked to possession in a material sense. What Moyles means by the term has more to do with the child taking control over finding the answer to a question that interests her. When you think about it, it begins to seem obvious that if the child has chosen what to do and how to do it then the child 'owns' the activity. And if you think even more carefully about children whose play you have noticed, you may realise that what made you take notice was the *deep involvement* and *intense concentration* of children engaged in play. So play – which is, by definition, self-chosen – is very likely to allow the child to become deeply involved and to carry on with the play for as long as seems necessary. But Moyles warns us that we – the adults – can very easily hijack the play and take away the sense of ownership from the child when we start to think that the best way of interacting with the child is to ask questions about what she is doing.

What do you think of this example, offered by a teaching assistant in an inner London school?

- Rahima and Joelle were playing with some dough which had been set out in the home corner. The teacher had put out some new kitchen tools – a potato peeler, a garlic press and plastic scoop. The two children (both aged four) ignored the materials because their play involved them using the dough to make 'money'. They were cutting it up into small and slightly larger pieces and then sorting these out into different sized bowls. They were very involved in making sure that they had three different sized 'coins' and their talk was mainly about that and involved words like 'same as', 'smaller', 'fatter', 'more than', 'costs' and so on. The teacher had her own learning goals for the children and these involved seeing how well they could use the different tools. She was looking at their development of fine motor skills. The children had been playing for well over 45 minutes when she came over to them and said, 'Have you used that lovely peeler yet?' Neither child replied. She persevered, 'Do you know how to use it? Shall I show you?' At that point Rahima grabbed Joelle by the elbow, whispered in his ear and the two went off to the book corner.

It is not difficult to see how this teacher, attending more to her own goals than to the children's interests, managed to take ownership of the activity from them. Practitioners must ensure that they find ways of being able to share the focus of the child's attention and not impose their own agenda on the situation. The consequence was that the children removed themselves from a situation which, minutes before, had been deeply interesting and rewarding to them.

One of the most significant thinkers of the last century was the Russian psychologist Lev Vygotsky. He, like Piaget, saw the child, from birth, as trying to make sense of the world and everything in it. For Vygotsky, the child was actively using all means possible to make sense of things – from the first objects or people encountered, to the ways in which objects could be used to represent other things, to relationships, roles, rules and groups. For him, play was certainly one of the most common and powerful ways in which children made sense of this world, and in his work he talked of play as 'imagination in action'. His views are important and complex, so we will spend a little time making sense of them. It was the imaginative aspect of play that made it such a powerful learning tool, in Vygotsky's opinion. For him, the criteria that made play distinctive was the fact that in play, a child creates an imaginary situation. His thinking around this is difficult, so be patient and read this carefully. In essence, what he was saying was that it is only when a child is able to move beyond what can be seen or felt or heard to what is imagined that we can call it play. The child becomes able to *move from the reality of the here and now to the what might be*. In other words, the child no longer has to depend on the visible or the actual, but becomes able to consider the possible through asking such questions as 'what if?' or acting in ways suggesting 'as if?' In this way the stick becomes a horse, the child adopts the stance and gestures of the teacher, the climbing frame becomes a palace, the blue scarf turns into a river and then a shadow. More than this Vygotsky argued that all play involves *rules*. These are rules that are not imposed on the play by others but arise from it and are *constructed by the player* or players. Let's look at some examples to make this clearer:

- Molly (aged 3), in the home corner, is playing the role of mum. She is very busy putting things on the table, talking to the dolls and dressing them. She is playing alone and drawing on her previous experience of watching what her mum does. The rules for this play revolve around what it is she has decided that mothers can and cannot do. Since she is playing alone she alone sets the rules.
- Tahime and Jaspia are playing together in the home corner. They are both 4 years old. They started off with some domestic or home play but later decided that they should turn the home corner into a cafe so that they could set up a tea party for one of the dolls. They decided to bring in an additional table, used some coloured paper to make table cloths for both tables, used the home corner plates and plastic glasses to set the table, arranged the dolls on chairs and are now discussing how to make a birthday cake. They use their previous experience about birthday parties to set up the home corner to resemble parties they have seen or participated in. The rules seem to be that the tables should look nice; there should be things to eat off and drink out of; the dolls should be present and sit round the tables and there should be a cake. They are negotiating the rules as they play.
- In the yard of the preschool, a group of children are involved in a complex sequence of play about a fire. The house next to Noludwe's house was burned down in the previous week. Many of the children live close together and so witnessed the fire. The children have no specialist equipment or expensive toys to support their play, but they have their imaginations and they choose to adopt different roles as the play moves ahead. Fikile and Noludwe choose to be people living in the house that is burning. Sam and Essie decide they will fetch the water to put out the fire while they wait for the fire engine. They take two buckets and some sticks, which become hoses to spray the water onto the pretend fire. The girls in the fire shout 'Help! Help! Save us!' and the play progresses at a furious rate. When the fire has been put out and both girls rescued Noludwe lies on the ground and shouts for a doctor. Yusuf joins the play and becomes a doctor. He uses his shoe lace and puts it round his neck and pretends it is a stethoscope. He listens to Noludwe's heart. 'You are going to die' he tells her solemnly. 'We are all going to cry'.

Then he waves his arms in the air and shouts 'Come on, everyone. We have to cry. Noludwe is going to die'. Here the children draw on their own first-hand experience to explore something dangerous and possibly very frightening – fire and death. The rules they generate relate to how they understand firemen will dress and behave and how those trapped will feel and seek help. The tragic ending involves Yusuf orchestrating a mass display of grief and sorrow. For these children grief and sorrow may well have been features of their lives.

One of the most important things about play as imagination in action is that it involves *children being able to use one thing to stand for or represent another*. This ability to turn a concrete object into something else is an essential part of all learning because so much of what governs our societies is abstract and coming to understand this is difficult. When a child uses a stick to be a magic wand, the child knows the stick is still a stick (the actual, the real, the visible) but can use it to act as if it were a magic wand or a horse or a light saver. Those are the magic words ... *as if it were*. So the child can behave as if she were a mother or a teacher, or dying or fighting, or happy or sad, or alone or in a group. The child can use the objects around her to be whatever she chooses or needs in her play and she can involve others in joining in this enterprise. This is the exploration of *symbols* and essential for learning.

Practitioners need to be alert both to how children use one thing to stand for or represent another and to the significance of this in beginning to become able to join communities of symbol users – for example readers and writers.

Vygotsky was clear that exploration was not the same thing as play and that was because, for him, play referred solely to imaginative play. But we have a broader definition of play, one that takes account of exploration and investigation and problem solving. So let us go to the work of Corinne Hutt to help us understand more. Hutt was aware that some theorists were saying that play was not the same thing as exploration, and set about studying this in depth. Her distinction between play and investigation centred round the notion that an investigating child seemed to ask *'What does this thing do?'* whilst the playing child asked instead *'What can I do with this object?'* Hutt was interested in looking at the concept of play being a mode of learning. For her, learning only really took place during exploratory behaviour. She used two terms to define the two different behaviours: *epistemic* behaviour related to finding out what an object could do and seemed to be concerned with knowledge and information – and significantly was goal-oriented; *ludic* behaviour was associated with finding out what the child could do and for Hutt involved self-amusement. In epistemic play the child had to concentrate on answering the question. Hutt divided epistemic behaviour into problem solving, exploration and *productive activity*. You know what problem solving and exploration are and what she meant by productive activity was acquiring a skill or skills or constructing something. So for her this kind of behaviour, brought about by the introduction of a new or novel object, was associated with new learning. Ludic behaviour is said by Hutt and her followers to be fanciful, imaginative and enjoyable and only takes place when the child is relaxed and in a familiar setting. It was her belief that any learning that took place was incidental. The implication is that the child would use what they learn through epistemic play in order to play in a fun or ludic manner. For us, however, ludic play involves the child exploring her or his own agency, ability to create things, to explore feelings, and develop relationships. These are surely vital aspects of learning.

Vygotsky might well have found this difficult to accept. He thought that the learning that took place in play – remember that for him it meant imaginative play – was so deep and serious that he said that 'In play a child is always above his average age, above his daily behaviour; in play it is as though he were a head taller than himself' (Vygotsky, 1967, p. 16). It is interesting to learn that when Hutt was involved in a project funded by the then DES (Department for Education and Science) which involved observing children who had been given a novel or new object to explore, she noticed that the children played in a serious, exploratory or experimental way before moving on to more light-hearted ludic play. She also noticed the difference that adult *interventions* in the play made. Now we have to be careful because adult intervention can be both helpful and harmful. It is difficult to do sensitively and, if not done sensitively with regard to what the child is interested in, it can destroy the play.

We arrive at another implication for practitioners. *Observing* children at play – watching them, listening to them, trying to find out what it is they are trying to find out – is the starting point for any intervention. The practitioner must empty her or his mind of any predetermined goal or target. The intervention must relate to what it is the child is trying to do or find out and not to what the adult wants the child to do or learn.

Barbara Rogoff is one of the relatively few writers or researchers to have done her work in cultures other than dominant Western cultures. Her interest is primarily in social groups and so her interest in play concerns what she calls *social play*. She is interested in what children do when they are on their own together without the presence of an adult. In her view the presence of an adult changes the dynamics of the situation. She is interested in the cognitive features of *peer interaction* (children in relation to other children) where there is no form of control. She believes that where children are not being controlled in any way they have the freedom to play with the rules themselves and to change the goals of any activity whenever necessary. She reminds us that much of the research on play (e.g. that of Piaget or Hutt) looks at what children do with something new on their own. Rogoff suggests that even where children play on their own, this may involve social practices as the children try out new ideas or roles or feelings without the pressures involved in more formal learning.

Rogoff is most famous for her view that most learning takes place through what she calls *guided participation*. This is where the child is in the presence of a more experience person, child or adult, and through observation and action behaves like an *apprentice* to the more experienced learner. When groups of children gather in the absence of an adult, the children need to decide what to play. They must *negotiate meaning*, which means they must agree on what it is they are doing, how they are doing it and so on. They must work together in order to maintain *intersubjectivity* – which means an understanding of the intentions and feelings of each other – in a play scenario that they, together, create. In her book *Apprenticeship in Thinking* (1990) she has a photograph of a group of children and young people in Guatemala who are cooking and serving a make-believe meal modelled on what they have been involved in learning to do in the real-life process of preparing meals. They have no access to toys and use leaves to make tortillas and dirt to make or represent meat. The children learned about cooking and serving meals through being involved in one way or another in the real lives of their communities, and in their social play act out what they have done in order to consolidate and refine their learning. One might be tempted to say that these children are learning in preparation for their future as Guatemalan women. There are some researchers who believe that play is not preparation for life but *a resource for participating in everyday life*. This idea – a communicative perspective on play – framed by Bateson (1973) is one that sits well with our definition.

To illustrate this, here is an example which comes from a research study carried out by Harriet Strandell and set in a Finnish daycare centre. It involves three little girls, all aged 5, who are playing together. Their play involves climbing on things and two of the girls are talking about furnishing their house. The third little girl, Liisa, listens to them and tries to join in by deciding what it is they would like her to do in order to be admitted to the play. Here is a small extract from what is said. (My comments are in parentheses.)

Liisa: This door must be kept closed.
    Liisa goes to close the sliding door. Then she returns to the corner.
    (Notice that Liisa uses her own initiative to try and establish what she
    must do in order to be admitted to the play scenario)
Liisa: Is it dark enough?

Anu: Shall we let Liisa come and play with us now?
Rita: No!

(Strandell, in Penn. P. 152)

Liisa is then presented with additional conditions for participation and at the end of the episode the other girls comment on the fact the she is not in their unit in the centre. 'Luckily you're a Ladybird! Luckily it's our turn!'

Strandell tells us that the girls are calling up a daycentre rule which allow different units the right to use particular areas at different times. Liisa would like to be able to negotiate as an equal with the others, but they use the play situation in order to exercise their power to exclude her.

This is not an exhaustive list of theorists. You will encounter the ideas of others throughout the book. The first of the case studies looks at the work of some of those who are perceived as being early pioneers of play.

Case Study 1 Early pioneers in play: a taster

The German educationalist Friedrich Froebel developed the first kindergarten where play was seen as the medium of education. The curriculum called for the manipulation of objects which he called *gifts*; children were engaged in craft activities which he called *occupations* and were also involved in games and songs which he called *mother's plays and songs*. He was essentially an idealist and his methods were aimed at enabling children to gain abstract ideas and spiritual meaning.

Maria Montessori designed materials especially for her early years setting and then observed children playing with them. She then abstracted what she regarded as the essential elements of play and built these into her programme. Her approach was essentially empirical and some question whether play was ever truly involved.

Rudolf Steiner's approach to education was largely based on play. He had a strong belief in the importance of play and drawing and storytelling in the early years. He believed that no child under the age of 7 should be taught to read and that children should be taught to write before they learned to read. He was interested in the links between art and science. His schools are still popular today. He is regarded as both an idealist and a pragmatist.

Susan Isaacs, with her focus on education, psychology and psychoanalysis, believed that children learn best through play. She believed that play should be viewed as children's work and that social interaction is an important part of play and learning. She regarded the emotional needs of children as being very important and said that symbolic and fantasy play may often be a release for a child's feelings. In The Maltings School she observed children carefully, took detailed notes of what they said and did and used this as proof of them as competent beings.

Rachel and Margaret McMillan were sisters who played significant roles in the development of nursery education in the UK. In 1914 they opened the Open-Air Nursery School & Training Centre in Peckham. Within a few weeks there were 30 children at the school ranging in age from 18 months to 7 years. After Rachel died Margaret continued to run the Peckham Nursery. She also served on the London County Council and wrote a series of influential books that included *The Nursery School* (1919) and *Nursery Schools: A Practical Handbook* (1920). The Rachel McMillan College was opened in Deptford on 8th May, 1930, devoted to the training of both nurses and teachers.

Summing up

Bruner saw play as both a process and a mode of learning. He talked of play being memory in action and recognised the importance of experience and cultural tools. He saw children as actively constructing meaning, as did both Piaget and Vygotsky. This reminds us to ensure that children have opportunities to draw on their previous experience.

Bruce talks of play as being an integrating mechanism and that again drew attention to prior experience and memory. Her work reminds us of the importance of knowing as much as possible about the children in our care in order to be able to understand what they are focusing on as they play.

Piaget's focus was on children constructing meaning through experience – in the earliest years through the physical exploration of objects. From this he said that children began to be able to form categories and develop logical thinking. His work on schemas reminds us that behaviour that may appear random is really purposeful.

Moyles's deep concern is with the importance of children retaining ownership of what they do in play. It is only when they are doing this that they are able to get deeply involved in what they are doing. This reminds us that we need to be sensitive in our efforts to appreciate what it is that children are paying attention to and that we find ways of sharing this focus of attention.

Vygotsky's work on cultural tools emphasised the vital role that the social and cultural play in learning. His deep interest in the use of signs and symbols and pretend play helps us see many children moving from the here and now to the possible. His interest in rules helps us explore rule-bound systems like writing and mathematics and music.

Hutt's work on play is complex and changed over time. It reminds us of the importance of agency and of the role of adults in supporting and promoting play.

Rogoff, with her work in the developing world, emphasised the importance of the context and saw children at play as being apprentice learners to more expert others in their communities, and showed how, in play, children have to negotiate meaning and roles.

Chapter 2

Taking inventory of the world

The purpose of this chapter is to explain how the human infant, from conception, actively seeks to make sense of the world, initially through using what is available – other people, language, their own senses and movement. The importance of others in this sense-making journey and early interactions between children and caregivers are explored and this leads into how children come to understand the intentions and the needs and the feelings of others. The human infant is seen as competent, communicative, questioning and playful as she explores everything she encounters in her world.

> 'Can you tell of childhood what is no longer known? Can you not describe but survey it in its magical states, recover its mystery of clay and clouds, of stairway shadows and mad wind, and bear witness to the enclosure constructed while, plucking off petals of mystery and dream, you were taking inventory of the world?'
>
> (Chamoiseau, 1993, p. 3)

At the beginning ...

A group of students were asked what they thought might be described as the earliest play of children. Their responses are interesting to read.

Ali: I think they play with the toys they are given. Baby toys. Things like rattles.

Mona: My baby played with my hair. Whenever we held him he put his fingers in my hair and played with it, feeling it. I think it comforted him.

Abiola: Babies at home in Nigeria often don't have toys. Many people can't afford them and the ones that are homemade are too sharp and dangerous for them, so perhaps they don't really play until they are older. But when I think about it they do play because they pick up things they find and put them in their mouths and shake them and things like that.

Evanthia: At my nursery we give the babies treasure baskets full of interesting things to explore. They are all natural objects – things like pine cones or bits of wood.

Peter: On my teaching course we were told that we could only call it play when children invented an imaginary world.

Selma: The first play – I think – is when the adult starts something that the child can join in with. In my family we do things like saying 'one for you and one for me' to get him to eat. It is also about taking turns. But my friend Angelina thinks it goes the other way round – that the baby starts something and the adult copies it.

Bea: My baby used to love putting a rag over his face and letting me pull it off. I thought that was his first play.

It is clear that people think very differently about what play is and about where it starts. For some, play starts through interactions with others; for others, it only starts in the presence of toys; for some, as soon as the infant tries to make sense of the world.

Technological advances and the development of imaging equipment allowing us to see into the human body have enhanced our understanding of how the human foetus develops. You will almost certainly have seen pictures of the foetus and read accounts of some of the things researchers have discovered about early development. It is generally accepted now that, at birth, the human infant already has experience on which to draw. We know that the foetus can hear in the womb both the sounds of the mother's body and external sounds such as voices and music. It is unlikely that sight is as highly developed because of the lack of light in the womb. But movement has developed, even within that confined space. At birth, when the child emerges into what William James called 'a buzzing, blooming confusion' she is equipped with some vital structures plus some experience on which to start the lifelong journey of making sense of that world.

Yet by the age of – let's say 4 years – the same child is able to identify people as being different from objects or animals and from one another and can recognise and name some people and animals and objects. More than that, the child can interact with others and respond to what they say or do, answer their questions, laugh at their jokes, even pay attention to their needs or fears. The child will recognise and use a table or a chair, or a brush or a broom, from whatever angle; feed herself using hands or spoon or chopsticks or knife and fork; perhaps dress herself, and both speak and understand her home language or languages. The child, in a very short space of time, has become a fully functional and competent member of her community. How does this come about? The neuroscientists Alison Gopnik and her co-authors ask 'How is it possible that children come to understand the minds of others, the outside world and language?' They call these 'the ancient questions' (Gopnik et al. 2001, p. 4).

Piaget, together with his wife, started recording the observations of the lives of their three children through keeping diaries of their daily behaviour. The records are detailed and chart in minute details the significant patterns in their behaviour. Piaget's work was original and insightful and he was the first person to suggest that babies actively seek to make sense of their world. They construct meaning. As a biologist, he was interested in both the physical and the intellectual development of babies. For him, thought referred to internalised action. You may well know that he adopted a *stage theory of development*, seeing children moving through different stages of development with age, and he believed that this early learning could be described as being *sensorimotor* (i.e. involving the senses and movement) in nature. This view is still to be found in many of the books on child development. But let us stop for a moment to consider if this is a full and adequate explanation of what happens after birth. In fact, most of the books you read about play talk about the first play as being what is called 'object' play. The question we want to ask is, 'Is that enough?' Since, according to our definition, all play is purposeful, surely the earliest play includes playing to understand not only objects, but people, events, rituals, customs, values, sounds, feelings and more.

No child is born into a vacuum. All children are born into a world which involves objects (the cot, the trees, the breast, the bottle, the birds); people (parents, carers, siblings, grandparents and others); customs (being pushed in a pram, carried on the back; put to sleep in a cot or a drawer or a basket; talked to, sung to, chanted to) and feelings (the pain of hunger, the comfort of warmth, the pleasure of interaction, the anger at being not heard). So whilst Piaget was right about children using what is available to them in order to make sense of the world, and recognised the importance of the environment to learning and development, he paid scant attention to what we might call the *cultural or social contexts* – by which we mean the routines and customs and values and beliefs and practices that are particular to different groups in society. Many theorists now believe that the context is essential to understanding both learning and play as a mode or way of learning.

Here are examples of some of such contextual features of experience:

- Here is Ola who is 3 months old. She is carried in a blanket on her mother's back as her mother makes her way to the market. She can see little because she faces her mother's body but she can hear her mother's voice as she greets people and talks to them about what she is purchasing. She can feel the warmth of the sun on her face or the breeze against her cheek. She can feel, too, the warmth of her mother's body and the security of moving with her mother as her mother walks. So although she is certainly using her senses to begin to understand the world, she does that within a context.

- Here is Thembo. He is also 3 months old. He is being pushed in a pram by his childminder. He lives in London and his mother is a student, completing her PhD. Miriam, the childminder, has been looking after him since he was 6 weeks old. She talks to him all the time as she pushes him to the park. What she does is describe all the things they are passing. He cannot see them since he is lying flat but he can hear her words and feel the movement of the pram and hear the traffic. 'Hey baby' sings Miriam 'it is raining again. It rains all the time in this place, but you are nice and dry and snug in your pram. We will just go and buy the milk and the bread and then go back home to stay dry.' Thembo is using his senses to start understanding the world and it is important to notice that the context in both examples involves two things which are very important to our understanding of play – the interaction between the child and other people and the use of language.

For both of these children it is clear that whilst their explorations certainly involve looking and listening and feeling and moving, they also involve the relationships they have with others in their world, their feelings and the language or languages of their homes.

Social, communicative and competent babies

Recently there has been much research examining what it is that babies know from birth. Using videotapes of human infants the research questions include:

(a) Do babies, presented with two things, think that they are the same or different?
(b) Do they express (not verbally, of course) a preference for one over the other?

Since babies are not able to use language, we cannot ask them these questions. But we can show them images of people or events and then assess whether or not they can differentiate between them.

Here is one such experiment. Babies were shown images of human faces and other images of objects including a complicated pattern – perhaps a chequer board. Then the researcher recorded the eye movements of the babies and analysed their findings. The research assumption is that babies will spend longer looking at the images that interest them (or that relate to what they have already experienced) than those that don't. And you will not be surprised to learn that the babies looked for longest at human faces.

In a related experiment babies were given dummies to suck and their sucking determined the length of time that either a videotape or audiotape of the face or the voice of the mother played. So the baby's action (sucking) determined the outcome. Sucking is satisfying for babies (as it is related to food in their experience) and children choose to continue sucking in order to prolong it and feel satisfaction when they are shown something that interests them.

As long ago as 1969 the Czech paediatrician Hanus Papousek presented his findings relating to his research into the head turning of infants. He was able to teach babies aged from 6 to 10 weeks to turn their heads either to the right or the left in order to turn on a display of lights which attracted their attention. Not only could the infants learn to do this but they could even be taught to turn twice to each side in order to produce the desired display. Over time they refined their actions so that they became able to turn only minimally to bring on the lights. More than that, they soon became used to the lights and only looked briefly at the display as though to confirm that they had come on. Papousek noted that the confirmation that their action had produced the required effect was often accompanied by a smile and he referred to this as a 'smile of predictive pleasure'. Bruner, reporting these findings in 1983, stated that what was significant about this was it seemed to show that infants could *predict* or anticipate that their actions would produce a change in their environment – a change that they found pleasing. Research like this shows several things:

(a) Babies shown repeated images over time get tired of them. (The technical term for this is *habituated.*) Shown endless happy face images they pay no attention when a new happy face is shown. But when a sad face is shown their interest is revived.
(b) From early after birth babies recognise the face and the voice of primary caregivers.
(c) They are able to discriminate between human faces and voices and other sights and sounds.
(d) They turn their faces towards a cloth that bears the scent of the mother's face.
(e) Before they can walk or talk, they show that they are attuned to facial expressions and tones of voice and human movement as opposed to other movement.

Early play

One of the things that characterises human infancy is the prolonged period of interaction between the infant and the primary caregiver, usually, but not exclusively or solely, the mother. Although play is evident in some other species, no other species demonstrates this intense *social and communicative interaction* which contains within it the beginnings of play as the search for meaning. Think, for a moment, of the games you have seen mothers and other caregivers play with infants. One of the most common is the game where something or someone is hidden and then revealed. In English, this game is known as *peek-a-boo*.

Here is an extract from a developmental diary made by a parent. It is about 5-month-old Sarah:

> Sometimes we play games after she's finished eating in the high chair. She loves one where I take a few of her toys, hide them under the table top shouting 'all gone' and then making them pop up again just after. She squeals with delight. I once dropped one of the three toys we were playing with by mistake and I could swear she looked a bit puzzled when we put only two toys back on her table.
>
> (Karmiloff-Smith, 1994, p. 173)

Here are some examples of mother/caregiver and child language and *predictive games* (i.e. games where anticipating what will happen is essential to the success of the game):

• Shahanara was sitting on her mother's knee and her mother was singing a song in Sylheti. At the same point in the song, each time it was sung, the child looked at her mother intently, clapped her hands and shrieked with joy.

• Hlengiwe's grandmother sang to the child before bed and at the same point in the song on every occasion pulled the child close to her and tickled her. Hlengiwe's anticipation of this was evident in the tension of her body.

• Leah was playing with her dolls and we heard her using a sing-song voice and a high-pitched tone as she talked to the dolls. 'No baby. Silly baby!'

In many culture there is a powerful element of tactile stimulation in the absence of objects in the play between adults and children. There is the Bengali game of Kan Dol Dol where the adult and child sit facing each other, each holding the other's ears as the adult (usually the mother) rocks the child and sings.

There are more such games and variations of them with similar themes in other languages and cultures. What these games have in common is that they depend to some extent on the use and the *exchange of language*. They also involve some prediction which requires the infant to come to know what will happen next. Bruner described these games as 'idealised' and talked of them having both a *deep structure* and a *surface structure* – terms he borrowed from Noam Chomsky, who wrote about language acquisition. The game is said to be idealised (or perfect) because the goal or purpose of the game is constituted by the game itself. Something is hidden and then revealed. All the actions lead toward the hidden object appearing. The game is made up of a set of acts or actions that are formed in sequence in a regular order. The game has rules and the sequence and consequence of the game can only be changed if and when the rules are changed. The goal of the game is the appearance and re-appearance of the face of the adult player or an object from behind a cloth or a screen accompanied by the voiced 'boo'. The players determine the sequence and the 'boo' might be any utterance indicating surprise.

For Bruner the deep structure is the controlled appearance or disappearance of an object or a person. The surface structure refers either to the props which enable this to happen or to changes in the timing of the acts. Bruner believes that the format is language-like which is why he borrows the language used by Noam Chomsky. Another essential feature of these games relates closely to language – the importance of the partners in the exchange *taking turns*. There is a hider and a hidden, but these roles can be exchanged. In speech there is a speaker and a listener and they take turns in order to share and make meaning. So, for Bruner, these games are what he calls 'protoconversations'. This is an interesting word to learn. The prefix 'proto' means initial or first and so a protoconversation means the first or earliest communicative exchange between an infant and another person.

Related to the appeal of the peek-a-boo type games, Gopnik et al. (2001) suggest that babies become almost obsessed by hide and seek type games and cite the example of one infant who hid the same ring in the same place seventeen times, each time finding it with great satisfaction after her chant of 'all gone'. So children, in their exploration of objects and often in interaction with others, explore hiding and finding, object permanence, causal relationships and the properties of objects.

Play with objects/things

In many of the books written about play much attention is paid to children's play with objects. There is much to think about in this early play and certainly it seems that all children in all environments and contexts do explore whatever is to hand from the moment of birth. From birth the child is looking and listening, feeling and smelling, tasting and moving her limbs and fingers and feet and head and eyes. Her initial exploration of objects around her comes about primarily through looking and listening and touching. She observes everything around her, above her, close to her and further away. She sees things that move and those that are stationary. She sees things that are colourful or monochrome, things that are big or small. She hears the noises of her immediate surroundings and the wider environment – traffic noises, the sounds of birds and animals, a fruit falling from a tree, women washing clothes in the river, human voices, music, tools, and laughter. All of this takes place in a context and the context almost invariably includes the presence of other people who interact with the child around the child's explorations. After a few months the child starts not only to respond to things but to act on them. She starts to reach for and take and to bang and to mouth and to drop and to throw. Bruner tells us that the human infant spends a lot of time in the constrained and familiar situation of the home doing the same things over and over again. A single act, he says, like banging, is applied over and over again to a range of objects. Everything the child can hold or reach is banged. Piaget described this behaviour as *intentional* and *systematic* rather than haphazard and random (as had been previously thought). And since it is systematic we might suggest that rules apply.

We know that very young babies begin to understand something about *cause and effect* – 'I do something, something happens'. We have seen something of this in the examples of babies sucking dummies or turning their heads in order to make something pleasing happen. Babies are learning not only about both cause and effect, but also about agency – their own ability to make things happen. And their learning becomes more and more subtle and defined over time. By the age of 18 months or older they are able to use one object in order to affect another. Gopnik et al. (2001) cite the example of babies being shown a toy out of reach and then offered a toy rake. It was only those babies of about 18 months of age who knew that they could use the rake to reach the desired toy. By the age of about 3 they are able to give explanations for things they think and observe. Here are some examples.

- Pumla, trying to reach a ripe plum hanging down from a branch, went to get a broom from the front of the house to knock it down. 'It was too high' she explained when her dad asked her why she needed the broom.
- David, playing in the water, couldn't get some dirt off his hand. He went inside to fetch some washing up liquid which he poured over his hand. 'I thought it would make my hands clean like the dishes', he told his mum.
- Carlina, playing in the yard, sorted piles of stones according to size. She then went to pick some large leaves which she laid out on the ground in a circle. She then placed her sorted stones neatly on the leaves. When her mum commented on how nice her arrangement looked, she nodded and added, 'I needed the leaves to put them on'.

Some writers suggest that as children play with objects or things they appear to be asking the questions: 'What is this thing? What does it do? What can I do with it'? We return to these questions and their implications in the next chapter.

- We need to recognise the importance of the *games and rituals* that are used within the families and communities of the children and develop a repertoire of these plus others we devise to use in our settings. The peek-a-boo games are just one example of many. We need

to understand the importance of repetition, sequencing, pattern, listening, prediction and turn taking.
- We need to see human infants and toddlers as *competent beings* and be aware of and respectful of all their attempts to make meaning.

The underpinning philosophy of the Reggio Emilia settings is extremely helpful here. They operate with a particular image of 'the child', seeing that child who, from the moment of birth, is so involved in developing a relationship with the world and so determined to experience that world that she develops a complex and intricate system made of abilities, strategies and ways of building and maintaining relationship. They call it a *pedagogy of relationships*. Carlina Rinaldi summarises this as follows:

- A child who is fully able to create personal maps for his own social, cognitive, affective and symbolic orientation.
- A competent, active, critical child; a child who is therefore 'challenging', because he produces change and dynamic movement in the systems in which he is involved, including the family, the society and the school. A producer of culture, values and rights, competent in living and learning.
- A child who is able to assemble and disassemble possible realities, to construct metaphors and creative paradoxes, to construct his own symbols and codes while learning to decode the established symbols and codes.
- A child who, very early on, is able to attribute meanings to events and who attempts to share meanings and stories of meaning.

(Rinaldi, 2006, p. 83–4)

This is a complex social, cultural and political outline of the child around whom the provision for children from birth to the age of 6 is constructed. The implications of this are clear in terms of various factors.

 The roles of adults are critical, particularly in terms of the following:

- being able to *make contexts* where children are enabled to use their developing skills;
- building a *culture of respect*, of interaction and dialogue, strong relationships and communication;
- ensuring that adults and children, or children and children, can *engage in dialogue, focusing their attention on the same thing and that there are no imposed external goals or targets*;
- having *high expectations of children* and helping them learn to reflect on what they have done and to work and play alone, in pairs, in small groups, in large groups, sometimes observed and sometimes hidden from view.

Culture and context

Colwyn Trevarthen (in an edited version of his 1995 paper) tells us that children have an innate need to live and learn in *culture* (which means within the customs and routines and rituals and ideas and artefacts of a group), and he says that this is as necessary for them as it is for fish to swim in the sea or birds to fly in the air. For him the essential human motivation is to understand the world and to do this by sharing experiences and goals with others through language and other cultural tools. He talks of how children seek to understand the world through 'sharing experiences and purposes with other minds' (Trevarthen, 1998, p. 87). The human infant then begins to be able to move away from the immediate – from the here and now – to the wider world, whilst still being able to refer back to her own experiences and interactions.

You will remember that the previous section ended with Bruner's assertion that games can be seen as protoconversations, and Trevarthen helps us to understand this more clearly. He says:

> Meanings ... are discovered in our community by people comparing, negotiating, and showing their interests to others. We can construct together only by allowing turns in initiative. These cooperative skills have a strong innate foundation, as is made clear by the way in which very young infants become involved in 'protoconversational' exchanges of expression with other persons, and by the rapid development of enjoyment in games in which events and actions on objects are made to be part of rhythmic expressions and their use is negotiated in interactions.
>
> (Trevarthen in Woodhead et al. (1998), p. 88)

So parents and carers, through the rituals and games and interactions between them and their babies, set them on the path of knowing how to take turns, how to predict, how to enjoy and how to understand goals, events and actions and to explore the roles that they can play. This is the essence of learning.

One of the most important aspects of this type of interaction is the ability of the two partners in the pair or dyad to *share the focus of attention*. This emerged initially through the work of Daniel Stern (1985). Soon after the baby is born it is evident that not only can the infant make eye-to-eye contact but can also sustain it. For the mother or primary caregiver, this is a staggering moment – the first real interaction and often the response of the adult is to vocalise or say something. By the end of the second month of life eye-to-eye contact with vocal accompaniment from both adult and infant has become well established. And what happens is a duet: adult and child taking turns, turning on and turning off.

Later, the caregiver begins to introduce objects between herself and the child and these become targets for joint attention. Bruner cites the example of 3-month-old Jonathan whose mother introduced objects in two different ways. The first was to put something between herself and her child whilst they were in eye-to-eye contact, and as she did so to make her utterances go up in pitch and stress. So she might say something like 'See the big *ball*' with a rising tone and emphasis on the name of the object. At the same time she moved the object into the child's line of vision. The second was to pick up an object the child was focused on and move it into the space between herself and the child and again shake or move the object as she commented on it.

The technical term for this sharing of understanding or focus of attention is 'intersubjectivity'. This term has already been mentioned in the first chapter. This originates in the mother/caregiver-child interaction, before the child is using verbal language and is, naturally, bathed in the emotional content of the interaction. Trevarthen (1998) tells us that smiles during mother/caregiver-infant play show that both mother/caregiver and infant are jointly experiencing joy or pleasure in the interaction and – more than that – are aware of one another's feelings of joy or pleasure. When language enters the frame, the mother/caregiver and child are able to share their responses with others: this is known as *secondary intersubjectivity*.

In her first novel, *The Bean Trees*, the American novelist, poet and human rights activist, Barbara Kingsolver, wrote about a poor Kentucky woman who became guardian to an abandoned baby girl. The child had been brutally hurt and abused and in a powerful scene early in the novel Kingsolver described one of their earliest interactions as she undressed the child for the first time and observed the terrible marks on her body.

All of the baby's clothes were way too big, with sleeves rolled up and shirt tails wrapped around and everything wet as mud boots and as hard to get off. There was a bruise twice the size of my thumb on its inner arm. I threw the soggy shirt in the sink to soak. The child's hands constantly caught my fingers and wouldn't let go. "You little booger," I said, shaking my fingers and the little fist. "You're like a mud turtle. If a mud turtle bites you, it won't let go till it thunders." I hadn't any sooner gotten the hands pried loose from my fingers before they grabbed onto my shirt sleeves and my hair. When I pulled off the pants and the diapers there were more bruises.

Bruises and worse.

The Indian child was a girl. A girl, poor thing. The fact had already burdened her short life with a kind of misery I could not imagine. I thought I knew about every ugly thing that one person does to another, but I had never even thought about such things being done to a baby girl. She sat quietly in the bathtub watching me …

The kid was splashing like a toad frog. Her fingers were wiggling and slapping at the surface of the water, no doubt trying to grab hold of something. "Here," I said, and handed her a washcloth that had BROKEN ARROW written on the selvage in indelible magic marker. She hugged that wash cloth and smiled. I swear to God.

(Kingsolver (1988), p. 23 (Virago edition 1990))

The narrator, Taylor, names the child 'Turtle' and this is the start of their long, shared journey through life. This has been included here both to suggest the power of early interaction and also the assumption by most of those interacting with very young infants that they are seeking to communicate their needs and fears and wants and thoughts. Taylor shows how her observation of the child's hands in the water together with the bruises on her body allowed her to guess that the child wanted something to hold onto.

Later in the novel the pair arrive at the home of Mattie, who clearly knew more about babies than did Taylor, and gave Turtle some peanut butter crackers to eat and juice to drink. In the next extract Kingsolver describes the interaction between Mattie and the baby, where Mattie understood what Turtle wanted and used just the patterns of speech described above by Bruner.

When she came back Turtle had drunk all her juice and was banging the cup against the tire, demanding more in her speechless way. I was starting to get embarrassed.

"You want more juice, don't you?" Mattie said to Turtle in a grownup-to-baby voice. "It's a good thing we brought the whole bottle down in the first place."

(Kingsolver (1988), p. 44 (Virago edition 1990))

The case study that closes this chapter comes from the work of Rogoff and describes the interactions and relationships between a toddler and his mother around an everyday experience. Here we see a small child displaying his competence in looking to his mother to validate his attempts to resolve a dilemma: was the play dough – so similar in texture to real dough – edible or not.

Case Study 2 A Mayan toddler makes sense of an ambiguous situation

A 20-month-old Mayan boy was trying to decide whether or not a play dough tortilla was edible. He had been patting the dough into a tortilla with his mother's help. This is what he did:

The baby broke off a tiny corner of the little tortilla he had made and held it up expectantly to his mother. She absently nodded to the baby as she conversed with the adults present.

The baby brought the piece of play tortilla to his mouth and, looking at his mother fixedly, he stuck out his tongue and held the piece of tortilla toward it, with a questioning expression. His mother suddenly bolted out her hand and snatched his hand holding the piece of tortilla away from his mouth, blurting out 'No! Not that!' The baby looked at her with a little surprise but was not disturbed by the clear message that the dough is not edible; he watched quietly as she laughingly put the little piece of dough back on the rest of the tortilla, put it back into the baby's hand and told him that it is not to eat. He resumed patting the dough contently.

(Rogoff et al. in Woodhead et al., 1998, pp. 230–1)

Summing up

In this chapter we have examined the early play of babies as they interact with others and encounter objects and events in their lives. We have begun to examine the importance of society and culture to development and to think of human infants as social, communicative and competent. We have paid attention to the early games that take place between infants and their caregivers and seen how important prediction, routine and rules are to these games and how they lay the foundations for much of the learning to come.

The implications for practitioners are to consider the importance of ensuring that examples of and opportunities for repetition, sequencing, pattern, prediction, turn-taking, language, routines and listening are built into the activities we offer and to respect children as serious meaning-makers.

Chapter 3

Agency and ownership

We now move on to looking at two aspects of what we have defined as play that makes it different from some other modes of making sense of the world and of learning. We examine here how children across the world move on from asking what something is and what it does to examining what the child herself can do with it. This brings in the important concepts of agency and ownership. Agency is the notion of the child being in control of what she does and ownership means that the child is able to develop her own concerns.

> '... man only plays when he is the fullest sense of the word a human being, and he is only fully a human being when he plays'.
> (Freidrich Schiller, 1759–1805, cited in Sutton-Smith, 1985, p. 64)

Defining terms

In this book the word 'agency' is used to refer to the child being active in all the processes involved in making sense of the world. It is important to define the word for our own purposes because both terms 'agency' and 'ownership' are difficult to use in a book about play which sets out to ensure that it adopts a stance which is determinedly not Western (or Northern) in approach. Both words are suggestive of things relating to individuality and possession: here it is important to make clear that they are not used in those terms. All children are part of a culture, a context and a community and this is where they play and learn. This is where they begin to ask questions and seek to find ways to answer them. This is where they construct their own theories and test them out. And they do this through interactions with others in their community and contexts – with their siblings and peers, with their parents and grandparents, with their teachers and other significant people. A question arises in the mind of the child and the child makes a decision to try to answer that question using whatever is available to her. Here are some examples of what we would call 'agency':

- Fukui comes into the nursery in a very bright and cheerful mood and goes immediately to the block corner where he starts to build two towers side by side. His key worker Saeko watches with interest, sitting close by, but not intervening. Saeko notes that Fukui builds the two towers at the same time, a block at a time on each, ensuring that they are identical. He works ceaselessly until the towers are of a height that satisfies him. Then he stops, steps back and admires them. He turns to Saeko and says: 'I have made the twin towers, you see'. Saeko is surprised at this and says: 'They are exactly the same'. 'Yes', says Fukui 'I needed them to be exactly the same and that is why I built them both together'. Saeko continues with the discussion, initiated by the child; 'What made you decide to build the twin towers?' 'Oh' replies Fukui 'my dad told me all about them and about the aeroplanes that flew into them long ago. I am going to get an aeroplane now and see what happens if I fly it into my towers'. (Observation notes)
- Four-year-old Graca has been given a toy piano by her grandma and some old song books and sheets of paper with musical notation on them. She has never seen things like this before and looks and looks at them and then takes them over to her grandmother and asks 'What are these?' – pointing to the notes. Her grandmother says 'They tell you which notes to play.' 'What are notes?' asks the child. (Personal observation)
- 'A three-year-old child is playing with a piece of wire. First he makes a bracelet and then, on the back of a chair, the wire becomes a horseman riding his steed, and finally it is transformed into the horse's ear'.

(Rinaldi, 2006, p. 117)

In each of these three very different examples you find the child trying to answer a question which has arisen in his or her mind. Fukui's question relates to something his father told him about – a real event and one which he is trying to re-create in his own terms. He is in charge of what he is doing. Graca's question arises from something unfamiliar and her way of answering the question is to ask an expert. She is in control of getting the information she needs. The child in the last example is using a piece of wire to become something else – in fact to become three very different things. Here we have an example of the child asking the question 'What can I use this for? What can I make this be?' As soon as the child begins to think about what she can do with something, what she can make something become, what changes and transformations she can make, she becomes an agent of her own learning. No one is telling the children in these examples what to do or how to do it. They are the agents of their own learning.

It is evident that ownership, in this context, is closely related to agency, but it is particularly important in the context of classrooms and settings where, very often, children have little or no ownership of what they do during the course of the day. Teachers and practitioners more often tell children what to do, how to do things, where to do them and sometimes even with whom. Children may have ownership of what they do in the playground, sometimes in the nursery, rarely in reception classes and almost never in other classes.

You will remember that, according to our definition of play, both agency and ownership are essential. If you cannot remember the exact words of the definition you can refer back to page 2. Essentially, the definition insists that we can call something play only when the child herself has chosen to do it for her own purposes – perhaps to answer a question in her mind, perhaps to express her feelings, perhaps just to experience something. If the child has chosen to do it, then we can legitimately say that the child *owns the process* (i.e. what she does and how she does it) and *possibly the product* (what she ends up with).

Here are some vignettes which you might like to read and decide whether you feel that the children involved are playing or following instructions:

- In the reception class the teacher, Julianna, starts the day by reminding the children of who will be doing what. She tells 'blue group' that they should play in the home corner. They dutifully go off into the home corner and once there, move around for a little while until someone comes up with a *play script* – a suggestion of what they might do. Billy gets out the tool box and says 'Why don't we fix everything in the house? It's all broken'. He takes out a plastic screwdriver and sets about 'tightening' invisible screws all over the home corner. No one else seems interested in his proposal and two of the girls start dressing up whilst a third sets the table. Billy goes and gets a piece of paper and starts writing things down on this. Martha asks him what he is doing. 'It's a list', he says, 'of all the work we have done this morning. We need to be paid, you know.' Martha calls Eppe and Reshada and tells them that Billy needs to be paid for his work. This is the turning point in the game as all the children in blue group get involved. Billy's mention of money and pay appears to have interested all the children in the group.
- Abdu is new to the nursery and finding it difficult to settle. He has English as an additional language and has been in Nottingham for only a few weeks. He can't seem to find anything to do that meets his needs. His key worker watches him closely for a little while and then takes him by the hand to the sand table and lets him watch as she buries some shiny things in the sand, talking to him all the time. He watches intently what she does and then, when she steps back from the table, he puts his hand into the sand and starts to search for the buried trinkets. It is impossible to say for sure what it was about this that helped Abdu feel safe enough to start playing. Perhaps he had experience of 'buried treasure' through stories or DVDs; perhaps it was that there was no

need for spoken language; perhaps it was the attention paid to him by one adult.

- The teacher needs to ensure that all the children meet the targets outlined in the Early Years Foundation Stage (EYFS) curriculum. She realises that there are some children who have not yet shown that they meet these targets so she takes them, as a group, in order to check that they can 'count reliably up to ten everyday objects'. On the table in front of them she sets out ten objects. These are a pencil, a rubber, a ruler, a small book, an orange felt pen, a pair of scissors, an empty glue pot, a plastic cup, a sharpener and small ball of string. She asks the children, in turn, to count the objects, allowing them to handle them if they choose. Two of the children quickly and accurately count the objects and are allowed to leave the table. Three remain. Two of these have English as an additional language and one is desperate to return to what he was doing in the water tray.

These are fairly crude examples, but all drawn from real practice. In the first example the teacher, by directing the children to the home corner, limits their choice to some extent. But since she doesn't tell them what to do when they get there, the decision about what to do and how to do it is theirs. We would suggest that it is only Billy who is really playing because he is clearly able to follow up an interest of his own (working with the screwdriver and being paid for his work). The others join in with his play script and in order to do this they have to compromise and negotiate, and perhaps through this will be able to develop interests of their own that arise. In the second example the sensitive and perceptive key worker plans something which might stimulate an anxious newcomer and sets up a situation to raise questions in his mind. We would say that Andre is being offered a context which invites him to play. In the third example the teacher is having to do something with the children which is clearly of no interest to them and she exacerbates it by offering them things to count that can hold no possible interest for them. She might have asked them each to find ten things in the room that they like and bring them to her so that she can see what interests them. She would have had a better chance of actually finding out what they know about her targets if she had turned the task into one which might both interest and challenge them.

Using one thing to stand for or represent another

Much of the writing about early play talks of play with objects. There is a danger in this of assuming that only infants who have specialist objects (toys, in particular) will explore them. The reality is that children explore everything they encounter, from natural to found or made or living things. Earlier in this chapter we met a 3-year-old who used a piece of wire and his imagination in order to transform it from one thing into something else.

You will all probably have witnessed young children doing this over and over again – the child who puts a plastic cup or a leaf on her head to be a hat, a wooden block or a stone to her ear to be a mobile phone, a stick waved in the air as a magic wand or trailed in the dust as a mark-maker or placed between her legs as a horse or aimed at an enemy as a weapon. This ability to make one thing stand for or represent something else is something universal and very significant in terms of human development and learning. When one thing represents another, we can say that it becomes a symbol and our world is so full of symbols that we take them for granted and rarely think about how cognitively sophisticated it is to be able to operate with symbols. As you read this, you are making sense of these black marks on the page in order to understand the ideas which are in my head. I am trying to share my thoughts with you and doing this through written language which is symbolic. For children to succeed in our education system, to be able to read and write and manipulate numbers and use tools and enter the non-concrete world of ideas, they need to be able to use and understand symbolic systems. And they do this through their play.

Gillian Allery (1998) offers us a wonderful example of a small child in a London nursery turning a ball into a baby and a bucket into a pram. No one has ever told this child to pretend the ball is a baby. He has chosen to do this possibly because there is a new baby at home, possibly because he has heard a story about a baby, possibly because he remembers being a baby. We cannot know what his motivation is. What we do know is that something about the ball made him think that he could use it to 'be' a baby. And when he made that ball into a baby, his emotional involvement with the ball/baby was total. When someone dropped the ball, his distress was palpable. He fed the ball/baby and wheeled it into the shade when he was called inside for lunch. The ball became his baby and he became its parent or carer. His emotional engagement was total; he was in charge of what he was doing and how he was doing it. On the surface, what he was doing might seem totally trivial and pointless. In fact it is extremely purposeful and significant. He was playing.

Signs and *symbols* are significant for all learners and the difference between a sign and a symbol is not always clearly understood. Some believe that a symbol resembles in some way the thing that it is representing. The child who uses the plastic cup or a leaf to be a hat must think that it in some way resembles a hat. And perhaps a wooden block or stone makes her think of a mobile phone. A sign, by contrast, does not look like the thing it represents. Letters and words are symbols and in English they do not look like the things they represent, although in some languages (like Mandarin) they may well do. So the word 'hat' no more resembles a hat than the similar shaped words 'bat' or 'cat'. Very early on children use symbols in their play. From this they move on to being able to use signs. This is the beginning of being able to deal with *semiotics* and the *abstract world* of alphabets and other symbolic systems. You will find more about this throughout the book.

Everyday and scientific concepts

You were introduced to some of the ideas of Vygotsky in the first chapter. His work is important to think about as we move into the realms of symbolic and imaginary play. Vygotsky saw learning as the journey from what he called *everyday concepts* to what he called *scientific concepts*.

Everyday concepts are the concepts that children encounter through their interactions and activity in the everyday worlds of home and community. As they play and interact with others they develop such concepts, which are sometimes also called 'spontaneous concepts'. These might relate to cooking or eating, going to the clinic or the market, being sick or herding the goats or helping make the tortillas, the birth of a baby brother or starting school, going on holiday or feeling hungry, and so on. In other words, through their interactions, and mediated by spoken language, children learn the concepts relating to their everyday lives. For Vygotsky and for others the strength of these everyday concepts is that they have arisen from *direct*, usually *first-hand experience* and have not relied on memory. Those of us involved in the care and education of young children know about this, even though we may never have used the terms 'everyday concepts' or 'spontaneous concepts'. We know about the importance of the experiences children have had at home and within their communities before coming to the setting/school, and outside of the setting/school.

Scientific concepts, by contrast, are those that arise through some type of instruction more often in a formal system of knowledge rather than through interactions in everyday life. The child, in a formal educational setting, is exposed to some of the abstract conceptual knowledge of their culture. A child in a school in Kenya, for example, may be learning about some abstract concepts in common with a child in Sussex (dark and light, perhaps, or long and short), but also some very different concept (uses of cow dung as fuel or the importance of clean water). Through interactions with a more knowledgeable person, adult or child, the learner is introduced to these more abstract and more general concepts.

Two important points arise from this.

(a) Children need considerable experience of everyday concepts – of having first-hand experiences of things which make sense to them and whose purpose is clear to them before they are expected to deal with the more abstract things involving signs and symbols – things like reading and writing.
(b) Children need interactions with others, both adults and other children, where both partners are focused on the same thing.

The implications for practitioners include:

- considering carefully what experiences they can make available to children that are based on their interests, will make *human sense* to them and allow them to draw on their previous experience;
- seeing that children can build a store of *first hand experiences* which will provide them with the essential foundations to later enable them to deal with more abstract learning;
- identifying what it is that a child is interested in and paying attention to and using this as the basis for any intervention;
- remembering how spoken language around a *shared focus of attention* can scaffold learning and help the learner move towards independence;
- finding ways of allowing the child to lead and to follow the child's lead or, as Rogoff (1990) says to '*lead by following*'. This is harder to do than it sounds.

Storying

Storying – creating, making, telling and acting out stories is one way of learning to follow the child. Our example comes from the work of Vivian Gussin Paley, a former nursery teacher, magical storyteller and author of many wonderful books charting children creating and enacting their own stories in attempts to explain their lives and concerns. The extract below comes from her book *The Kindness of Children* (1999). She is visiting what she calls a London kindergarten where she meets Caroline, who is making up and dictating her own story.

> One day a little girl and a little boy went to a big forest but they didn't know if it had bad things or good things. It was a brother and a sister … So there was nothing that was bad. But they didn't know if there was. … Now Caroline must decide the fate of characters she herself has brought into being. Will she carry them to safety or allow them to suffer? My pencil awaits midair but Caroline is silent. After a few moments I ask 'Shall I read your story back to you? To see if you want to say more?'
>
> I review the text, pronouncing the final sentence slowly. 'So there was nothing that was bad but they didn't know if there was'. Caroline shakes her head; the story is done. She does not leave the table, however, wanting to hear the other storytellers. What will she learn from their privation visions and public disguises?
>
> 'The cat smelled the flowers and the dog smelled the leaves but they didn't smell the owner. Then he came.'

'A bat went up to the moon by himself. No one would help him. Then he found a spaceship.'

'The egg cracked open and the baby dinosaur looked and looked but he couldn't find his mum. Then his dad came'. …

It is Jordan's turn to tell a story. 'The little frog had no one to play with. They didn't like him. His leg wasn't long enough and he didn't jump proper'.

Involuntarily I glance at Jordan's legs, unable to tell if he can 'jump proper'. Young storytellers, of course, are well versed in the use of metaphor, but something tells me Jordan knows something of the frog's dilemma.

Caroline is interested in Jordan's story … (She decides she would like to finish it so Paley retrieves her paper from the pile on the table.)

'I fed my cat tuna fish' she begins. 'His name is Gus. I was three when I did it, in my old house. Then when I got down off my stool, Gus got up by my left and rub rub rubbed my leg. 'Cause we were so happy that time.'

'Is this still about the brother and sister in the forest?' I ask.

She is surprised by my question. 'Gus is in the forest' is her quiet reply.

I smile at Caroline, imagining the feel of a warm kitten. Even the youngest of these schoolchildren understand why Gus has to be in Caroline's forest. Other things will be there too, some in the shadows and some in the sunlight. That is why we keep telling our stories, so that inevitably we will arrive at the good part of the forest.'

(Paley, 1999, pp. 114–17)

The context that has been set up here is that of making and telling and sharing stories. Many practitioners will intuitively tell and share stories and some will invite children to do so. The teaching or *pedagogy* they are adopting may be described as being playful in the sense that the children are enabled and invited to make up *narratives* without having to write them down, and to do this for their own purposes and in play either alone or with others.

In the famous nursery schools in Reggio Emilia practitioners set up contexts which are responsive to the observed interests of the children. Here are some of the 'themes' that arose out of this:

• A discussion between a group of 4-year-olds led to work on eyes.
• A child came into the school and talked about a programme and that he – and many of the other children – had been watching on television. It contained images that some children – and many of the adult practitioners – found disturbing. To challenge and build on this the children and their adults began to think about images of other beings.

- In the town square, which is a regular meeting place of the people of Modena, there are stone lions. They are part of the everyday lives of the children, who climb on them and play on them. Lions were created and re-created in clay and paper and junk and colour. Children dressed as lions and played lions and made stories about lions.
- Children's interest in puddles on the way to school became an interest in reflection, in wetness, in the effects of splashing, in light, in colour, in mirroring; in drops and drips and running water.
- A child re-enacting a familiar rhyme involving bobbing a doll on her knee led to a project on horses and involved turning brooms into horses, making up stories involving horses, thinking about three-dimensional objects, running and riding and jumping. It led to examining words and their meanings.
- Children's interests in their shadows observed outside led to a project on shadowiness. The project that followed included uses torches, trying to catch shadows, moving on to talking of the shadow of death, thinking about protection, making and using shadow puppets, noticing how shadows change on a slope or with time of day.

In a day nursery in Ghana some very different themes were observed, although you may be interested to notice some common threads.

- From watching some of their parents in the fields, the children started to ask questions about roots and this became an ongoing theme as plants were planted and dug up, some root vegetables were collected and then cooked, children took care of the vegetable patch and talked about when it might rain, what sunlight did and so on.
- A child's mother died and the teacher in the setting noticed that some of the children were re-enacting funerals and talking about death. After a long discussion with the headteacher and the child's grandmother they set up a hospital corner in the room.
- Two of the children got a new TV and were really excited about it and so the group got involved in making a TV for the classroom out of an old box and then designed their own moving pictures using rolls of discarded paper. They were very ingenious and inventive.
- The children came across the word 'pair' in their class. The language of the school was English although most of the children spoke Hausa as their first language. They struggled to understand its meaning and so the adults decided to launch a whole topic about pairs.

The case study that closes this chapter comes from Alaska and explores one of the customs of the Inuit people, together with rules associated the custom. It brings to mind many similarities and many differences between and within cultures.

Case Study 3 From Alaska: storytelling with rules

In many countries there are rules around storytelling. You may well be familiar with the 'Crick-crack device', where the phrase is used as a signal to the listeners that a story is about to begin. You will know that many traditional stories in English start with words like 'Once upon a time' or 'Long, long ago' and end with 'And they lived happily ever after'. There are rules applying to the conventions of how listeners are drawn into the story and conventions around the type of language and language patterns that appear in stories. Stories for younger children often have a repeated refrain, inviting the listeners to join in and become part of the telling.

In Alaska there is a convention around storytelling common among the Inuit people living there. Most commonly it is the young girls between the ages of six and twelve who become storytellers. They are often accompanied by 'tagalongs' – younger siblings who sit and watch and are inducted into the rules of what deMarrais et al. (1994) call 'meaning making in mud'. Storytelling, in this culture, is seen as a vital part of retaining kinship patterns, reinforcing gender roles, building the oral tradition and maintaining cultural norms and values. More than that, it is seen as a vital part of learning as there is evidence in the stories of children using observation, spatial relationships, sequencing, classifying, predicting, solving problems, and memory skills. The links with pretend play are clear. Nowadays the custom has largely been replaced by watching stories on television and films, but girls still gather on the banks of the Kuskokwim River in mild weather to invent and tell their tales. The storyteller has to tell and illustrate her story and she does this by using a dull, flat knife which is pressed into the mud to make marks as she speaks. Each mark is erased and replaced by a new mark. The ritual is known as storyknifing.

Some aspects of storyknifing are interesting and relevant to thinking about rule-governed behaviours like pretend play and story making. The sessions always start in a similar fashion with the girls preparing their places, and moistening and flattening the mud so that it is the consistency they prefer for mark making. This is followed by bidding for who will start the story session and this comes about through the asking of questions, such as 'Who has a story?' or 'Do you remember when...?' Someone volunteers and the others listen intently, often stroking their knives as they do so. When the first storyteller finishes the next one starts and the sessions can last for over two hours. There seems to be some shared understanding that a session has finished and this is signalled by one of the older girls writing the word 'yes' in the mud. Each storyteller had a unique way of writing this word.

Researchers like Ager (1980) talk of three influences in the stories created by the girls. These are *traditional tales* they have heard and which usually contain moral, biographical or autobiographical accounts of real everyday events in the lives of the girls, and *introduced* stories which often draw on what they have learned at school. Embedded in the storyknifing session are also games and designs. One of the most common of the games is one called 'Guess whose house this is' where a storyteller draws the plan of a house together with furniture and the others have to guess whose house it is. The rule is to try and draw a house that no one recognises because no one has ever visited it. Another game involves writing words and disguising them by writing one letter on top of another or of reproducing the patterns used by garment makers in the community in their garments.

The reason for looking at this in such detail is not only that it is fascinating but also because it shows so clearly the importance of stories in the learning of people in this oral culture and shows how storyknifing like pretend play can reinforce cultural traditions, values and skills.

Summing up

In this chapter we have looked at the importance of the child being able to choose what to do and having ownership of what she does. In doing this we return to our original definition of play and emphasise that it is only when the child has agency that we can call it play. We have extended our earlier discussion of play with objects to looking at how children begin to use one thing to stand for or represent another, and this marks the beginning of our consideration of signs and symbols. We have looked too at the ideas of everyday and scientific concepts to refine our understanding of what experiences are important in the early years. Finally in this chapter we looked at storying as a way of enabling us start following the lead set by the child.

The implications for practice include ensuring that we think carefully about providing experiences for children which allow them to build on their previous experience, which make human sense to them and that relate to their observed interests. We need to find ways to enable us to know what it is the child is interested in or paying attention to so that we can share the focus of attention and sometimes use spoken language to scaffold learning. Most difficult, but essential, is learning to follow the lead given by the child.

Chapter 4

Memory and its role in play

This chapter is very much an extension of the previous chapter in the sense that we continue our examination of signs and symbols to begin to look at semiotics, the role of memory, the use of cultural objects and tools and the induction into groups, community and society. We continue our shift of focus from the individual to the cultural.

> 'In those early amorphous years when memory had only just begun, when life was full of Beginnings and no Ends and Everything was For Ever… .'
>
> (Arundhati Roy, 1997, p. 2)

Memory and experience

In the first chapter we touched on the links between play and memory when we thought about Bruner's consideration of play being 'memory in action'. Much has been written about memory by Bruner and also by Vygotsky and, more recently, by Alison Gopnik and her colleagues. Memory will certainly mean something to you as what we might call an everyday concept. It is the process of being able to call up things that have already happened. We all have memories and we all talk about both long- and short-term memory. And we might all agree that our store of memories has been built up of the experiences we have had.

Since we live in social worlds, other people are intimately involved in our experiences and hence in our memories. What children do, as they make sense of their world, is to use whatever means are available to them in order to understand each new experience in terms of other remembered experiences. Gopnik et al. tell us that even very young babies appear to have *representations* (or some sort of images) of the world which take the form of symbols in their minds. Infants, paying attention to all that is around them, take in information in the form of light waves and sound waves. It seems that children are born with a mechanism which allows them to turn the information gained into some sort of representation. Seeing a range of human faces in the days after birth the infant begins to build a representation of the layout or format of the human face – an oval shape with two marks symmetrically placed in the upper third and one larger shape in the middle of the lower third. Hearing a range of voices children begin to tune particularly into the voice most closely associated with gratification – that of the primary caregiver. We can infer this from the fact that there are experiments which show that very young babies respond to displays which remind them of the layout of the human face; that they recognise the voice of the mother or primary caregiver; that they follow moving objects with their eyes.

Remember that the human infant is born into a busy and complex world: there are people and the sounds they make; trees and natural forms and the patterns they create as parts move or the light shifts; faces that change expression; objects with complex structures and more. What is extraordinary is that the babies don't make simple exact representations of all they experience: the representations they make are both abstract and emotionally linked. All of this helps infants do some very sophisticated things. Gopnik et al. tell us that babies make representations that are rich and complex. For example, they may have ideas about how their face might resemble other faces, about how objects move or how the sounds of a language might be divided. Their representations may also be abstract as babies give evidence of linking information from different senses. For example, they might link the way the tongue feels and looks or the bounce of a ball and the sound it makes. More incredible is the fact that the representations they make go beyond sensation to include things like emotion (Gopnik et al. (2001), p. 145).

We can summarise this like this:

(a) Babies pay attention to some things and ignore others.
(b) They become habituated to some things and then ignore them. They are inviting change and stimulation.
(c) They form expectations and predictions.
(d) They begin to see similarities and differences.

Gopnik et al. suggest that this is all because the human infant is born with the capacity to form images through experience and interaction. It is this capacity to form images which is the basis of memory and which allows the child to start understanding the world from birth.

What follows are some examples of children at play and each has been selected in order to try to illustrate the role of memory in the play. As you read each example, link it to what you can assume about the prior experience the child or children concerned remember and are drawing on. Then examine the role of the adult and think about what this tells you about her relationship with the child.

The first example comes from Canning (2007) pp. 7–8:

> … a child is playing in the home corner. She is involved in pretend play, with all of her soft toys sat around the table. She is making them afternoon tea, they each have a tea cup and a saucer placed in front of them and she is pouring tea from a teapot and having a conversation with her toys as she serves each in turn. The adult is close by and the child calls out 'I'm having tea with my friends, would you like to have tea too?' the adult stops what she is doing and replies, 'Oh yes please, I've been gasping for a cup of tea all afternoon'. The adult goes over and sits at the table alongside all the toys.
>
> The child goes to get an extra cup and saucer, and the adult calls out, 'I really enjoy having afternoon tea, but I am afraid I have a problem'.
>
> 'What's that?' she responds.
>
> 'Well, it is a bit embarrassing; I can only drink my afternoon tea if it is served in a red cup with a matching red saucer'.
>
> 'That's OK', replies the child, 'I've got red cups in here somewhere', and continues to hunt in the cupboard.
>
> 'Does anyone else here have that problem?' The adult addresses the toys sat around the table.
>
> 'No, but look, Spot the dog has a matching green cup and saucer' the child replies for the toys.

You will have noticed that the child initiated the activity, that she draws on her previous and possibly considerable experience of tea parties. She knows how to handle tea pots and tea cups, how to seat 'people' around the table, what to offer and the appropriate language to use. She can only know all this from prior experience. She also responds to the very adult intervention in an appropriate fashion, indicating that she is used to being spoken to by adults as an equal.

 The implication for practitioners is that we can consider joining in play by becoming a play partner, and certainly by ensuring that we engage in real dialogue relating to the play with the child.

Let's look at a very different example of memory in action:

> Three little South African boys – Mpho, Sixpence and Tobias – have set up a stall in the outside area of their crèche. They place two old barrels a few feet apart and lay a plank of wood over them, to be their counter. Then they go inside and return with some worn plastic fruits and vegetables. Mpho says 'Let's get Zoli and Thando to make us some bread we can sell'. They go inside and fetch the two girls who happily agree

to make bread and set about doing this by making some mud cakes. 'What else?' asks Sixpence. 'We've just got bananas and guavas and onions. And that bread. What else can we sell?' 'Let's get some leaves and we can make those into bowls so it looks nice, like the one near my house. My next door neighbour sells fruit on the pavement' says Thando.

The practitioner comes out to see what the children are doing. 'Hey, it looks good! Do you want some of my plastic bowls and a sheet you can put on the ground like the sellers in the market?' The children are delighted with this suggestion and collect the offered bowls and plastic sheet. Then they call for the other children to come and shop.

(Personal observation, South Africa 1998)

You can see how the children here are drawing on their experiences of shopping in a much poorer community. They are familiar with market stalls and pavement sellers and this is what they re-create in their play. The two little girls know how to make dough for bread and use what is at hand in order to do that.

 The implications here are to ensure that we pay careful attention to what children are exploring, and possibly offer additional resources to extend their play and thinking.

The important point about additional resources is that care needs to be taken in deciding what to offer and why. You may have come across the work of McVicar Hunt. He had an interest in human intelligence and came up with a theory that became known as the Theory of Match. He believed that when children's play became repetitive, it was important for the educator to offer something new or novel into the situation. It was his belief that the novel object should be similar to an existing object in the play situation and not something completely different. The child, he said, needed to be able to make a link between her current experience and the new object. An example makes this clear.

Two children had been playing in the water tray over several days. One of the crèche workers noticed that the play was becoming repetitive and almost static. The children were just pouring water from one container into another. The worker decided to make a hole in the base of one of the containers and watch what happened. The children's play became more animated and they talked a lot to one another about the fact that 'water keeps coming out of the hole'. Two days later the worker put two additional holes in the same container and watched the changes to the play. A week later she added a sieve, a tube and a container missing any base. You can guess what happened.

Memory and role play

Do you remember the example of Vivian Gussin Paley at the end of the previous chapter inviting young children to tell and share stories? Children encounter stories told, chanted, sung, read or viewed and they also invent their own *narratives* (or stories) as ways of making sense of the world. They hear people around them telling stories in the form of descriptions of past happenings, plans for the future, overheard adult conversations, voices on the radio, gossip and talk on the phone and, if they are lucky, stories told and read. Many children throughout the world encounter stories and narratives also on screens, television, DVDs, videos, radios, play stations, computers and films. In her writing, Marion Whitehead (1997) claims that we all have an urge to hold onto and repeat or remould or re-enact something that has happened and in this way we give an ordinary event shape and pattern and this gives it significance. And so we find children playing out roles and, in doing this, shaping narratives, trying out roles, inventing rules to hold the play together, negotiating with others, sequencing events, deciding outcomes and perhaps making visible and audible what is in their heads. Watching children engaged in role play is an absorbing and fascinating thing to do. Here are some examples:

- Twenty-month-old Duncan toddled round the living room waving his mum's fish slice at every object he saw, muttering 'issy, issy, issy'. This activity carried on for more than twenty minutes and his mother concluded that he was casting spells on objects and in doing this was recreating a wizard he had watched on television.
  His narrative is casting spells; his inspiration what he has seen on television (Beetlestone, 1998).
- Three little girls are playing with the washing machine in the home corner of the nursery. Ola announces that she is washing the baby's clothes when Rahima interrupts saying she is the mum and this is her job. Alice challenges this, asserting that she is the mum. Ola hands over the clothes and decides that she will put in the washing powder. Rahima decides to go off and feed the dolly. Ola then decides to be the dad. This is an example of a shared play script, with the partners negotiating (not always happily or successfully) the roles they will play. In this domestic narrative potential conflict is over the role regarded by the children as the most significant – that of the mother (Sayeed and Guerin, 2000).
  Their narrative relates to everyday life in families as the children jointly try to make sense of family roles and tasks.
- On a beach an English toddler spotted another and bigger child and raced over to this child and began to talk in English. The older child was Greek and tried to explain to the small boy that he could not understand

what he was saying. But he picked up a stone to skim over the water. The smaller boy watched intently and tried to copy the actions. The sequence of taking turns at throwing stones into the water lasted for a while, until the older boy picked up a stick and started to scratch in the wet sand. Again, the little boy watched and copied. After a short time the older boy went off to talk to his mother and returned to offer the little boy a biscuit. At that point both children sat on the sand happily eating their biscuits.

This can be described as a shared but wordless narrative possibly exploring how to communicate in the absence of spoken language.

(Personal observation, 2009)

For Vygotsky *role play* – where children adopt roles and invent rules to explain the behaviour of the roles – is real, authentic play. For him, play with objects, predictive games, exploratory play were all just part of everyday life. It was the move to the pretend that made him come to regard play as such a powerful mode of learning.

In the earliest observed role play children adopt the domestic roles they encounter in their everyday lives within the family or community. They play at being mum or dad or baby or grandma or sibling. They may then move on to what is called functional play where they try out the roles of significant figures in their lives and communities – perhaps the teacher or the doctor or the imam. The development from there is an exploration of less real and more imagined or imaginary roles. You can read more about this in the next chapter.

Memory and semiotics

Semiotics is the study of signs and symbols, particularly as elements of systems of communication, such as language. It is very much concerned with meaning-making and with how elements of language, being rule-bound, allow those hearing it, speaking it, reading it or writing it to make and share meaning. The term 'language' in its broadest sense here to refer to spoken, read and written language, but also to those 'hundred languages' Malaguzzi talked about. It is important that semiotics, although commonly thought of in regard to language, is really about communication and what allows us to do this. The artist who uses colour and shape and space and line is able to communicate with those who see her work; the physicist who uses the symbols of mathematics and the specialised language of physics allows others (well, some others!) to understand her work; the signer in the theatre who uses the specific visual language of signing enables those with a hearing loss to make sense of what is taking place on the stage. All of these – and many, many more – are languages and all use signs and symbols and all are about communication.

We have talked about how young children come to use symbols when they use one thing to stand for or represent something else, and also about how children build representations of things they experience and store these as memory. Where children are offered access to systems of symbols (alphabets, numerals, musical notation) to use in their play they are able to ask questions and seek answers about these systems just as they do about all other aspects of their lives. Here, to illustrate this, are some examples of practitioners providing contexts to encourage this type of exploration. In each case consider the following:

(a)   the initial stimulus or starting point for the play;
(b)   the effect, if any, of resources found, made or supplied;
(c)   the links to previous experience; and
(d)   the evidence of children using semiotics in their play.

Context 1: The Kenyan general election 2008
The stimulus
Bame decided to set up a polling booth in the classroom just after the general election in Kenya. The time right after the election was one of fierce divisions in the country and he noticed growing factions developing even in his class of 6-year-olds.

The effect, if any, of resources
The school was in a poor region and had very limited resources, but Bame realised that he could get the children involved in making voting slips and slogans and even ballot boxes. In his opinion the very lack of resources meant that the children were actively involved in all aspects of the process from the very start of the project.

The link to prior experience
These young children had clearly not ever been actively involved in any aspects of a general election before, but aspects of the situation were familiar. They understood about why and how to persuade someone to choose one thing or person rather than another. They were used to making choices.

The evidence of semiotics
The children had to think about what needed to go on voting slips and in slogans, and in doing that they needed to use written language.

Bame's analysis of the play

'It was very successful. I noticed how much the children had to say when they wrote slogans or when one or two even wrote statements inviting people to vote for them. What they were able to draw on in this was their life experience of being unfairly treated, being poor, not having access to some of the things they wanted. Those who could not write very fluently got me to write for them. They dictated and I wrote. It was really a very moving experience for me.'

Context 2: Children peer teaching one another
The starting point
After reading a piece by Charmian Kenner on peer teaching a Year 1 class teacher, Mia, in a school in Reading decided to try and set up a peer teaching situation where children who were speakers of other languages taught one another things about these, their first languages. She had noticed just how much these children knew about their first language writing systems. What she had not expected was that the children should reproduce much of what happened in the initial session in their own play.

The effect, if any, of resourcing
This was a well-resourced school and teacher found she needed little in the way of resources other than a whiteboard, paper, pens and other graphic materials. It became apparent that what mattered in the play that followed the initial demonstration session was the process of teaching one another.

The link to prior experience
Clearly the bilingual children were drawing on their vast home and community experience of seeing their first language in print, seeing more expert people in their communities writing and reading the language and at least five of attending complementary schools to learn this language.

The evidence of semiotics
Semiotics was the foundation of the play that followed the initial session since all the children took turns at 'teaching' one another about features of their own writing systems.

Mia's analysis of what happened:

'I was delighted with the initial teaching session where the two children I had chosen were able to teach the others about some of the features of their languages (Bengali and Urdu). I was astounded that in the days that followed many of the children carried on teaching and learning about written languages in their play. They did this mainly in the book area of the classroom but I also saw some of it taking place in the playground. I also heard the children making wonderful comments in their play and afterwards. For example, David said: 'My language is English and it doesn't have curls and dots like Mohammed's language', and Isabel commented that she liked writing Bengali letters but that it was hard to get the line over the top to look right. Tamar said that Greek letters were more pointy than English letters and Elan insisted that he has to read and write his language (Hebrew) back to front. Well, back to front for us but the right way for him.'

Context 3: The building site in Rajasthan
The starting point
In Rajasthan, when work on the building of a new room for the preschool was complete, the children told their teacher, Archana, that they wanted to set up their own building site.

The effect, if any, of resources
The children had been watching the builders over a long period of time and they knew that the builders had used tools and signs to warn people of danger. There were few tools available to them but with the help of people in the local community they were able to borrow a spade, a wheelbarrow, two hard hats and some planks of wood. They were invited to make some signs of their own.

The link to prior experience
All the children had witnessed work on a very personal building site – which became their classroom.

The evidence of semiotics
Most interesting was their interest in signs and attempts they made to convey a message through a symbol.

Archana's analysis of what happened:

'I knew that the children were really fascinated by all that they saw when the builders were on site. They asked endless questions about every single thing that was new to them. Why did the men wear hard hats? Why were some of the signs triangular in shape? Where do bricks come from? Dozens and dozens of questions. We actually made a book about all their questions. And the signs they made were just remarkable. Iqbal made a triangular red sign with a wheelbarrow on it and asked me to write the warning message "Don't get wheeled over"; Pritha made a circular red sign with a hard-to-decode symbol on it. She said it was there to show that there were people at work and that the symbol showed "hard work". I am using that symbol in my class now to give to a child who has really worked hard!'

The implications are clear and many are things we have already said. We need to do the following:

* pay attention to what children are thinking, seeking to find out, doing and enjoying in order to *set up specific contexts*;

- analyse the contexts we set up to see if they are meaningful to the children in the sense that they can see the purpose of the contexts and draw on their *prior experience*;
- include materials to *stimulate mark-making and other ways of communication* in these contexts to stimulate and promote the use of signs and symbols in play.

Memory and cultural tools

Vygotsky, with his particular interest in the social and the cultural, spent much of his short life looking at learning in the context of culture. You will know that human beings have developed many different ways of communicating their thoughts and ideas about the world, often using signs and symbols in their communicative systems. Vygotsky believed that as we develop ways of communicating through cultural tools these very ways of communicating change our thinking and understanding. For example, think about how seeing a film (which is not reality but a series of moving images, sometimes bound by language and used to represent aspects of reality) can sometimes change what you think about something. The film is an artefact built up of signs and symbols. The same thing might happen through reading a book or talking to a friend or going to a lecture. So the ways of communicating or cultural tools change the ways in which we think. One of the most important things about cultural tools is that they allow us to think about things when the things themselves are no longer present. Here, then, is the link with memory. We can remember a film we watched in the cinema last night, or a book we read last summer or a talk we had with a friend weeks ago. We also develop tools to help us remember. Think about shopping lists, or mnemonics or notes stuck on the door of the fridge.

Here are some examples just to illustrate this point:

- Martha is about to go to the supermarket. She has a lot to buy and she makes herself a list to ensure that she remembers everything.

She is using the cultural tool of writing (developed by man over decades and used to facilitate memory and learning) in order to remind her what to buy.

- Parveen is new to the nursery class. He spends part of each day of his first week wandering around the perimeter fence of the garden saying out loud 'Here is the road. This is the corner. There is the climbing frame. Now I am on the grass. Here is the gate'.

Parveen is using the cultural tool of speech (developed and refined and elaborated by man over generations) in order to help him become familiar with a new and potentially threatening environment. He could equally well have drawn a picture of the nursery or just talked to his mum about it. Both also use cultural tools (making a pictorial image or using the spoken word) to mediate his learning of a next context.

- Xian is learning to play the recorder and has to learn to both name and play the notes written in the treble clef (in musical notation). In order to remember the names of the notes that sit on the lines of the treble clef Xian is given a mnemonic device by his older sister: EGBDF – every good boy deserves food.

Xian is using a mnemonic (a psychological tool for remembering, where the initial letter is used to stand for a word in a sentence, based on the idea that remembering something with a meaning is easier than remembering merely the names of letters). He has learned this from his older sister who, no doubt, learned it from another more experienced learner.

All of this takes place through interaction between people and Vygotsky believed that meaning-making took place through the process of what he called *mediation*. Put very simply, this is where a more experienced person (who could be the teacher, the practitioner, the parent, an older child, or even just a more experienced child) can help the child as a new learner to make meaning through the use of cultural tools (which could be spoken language, books, pictures, measuring, counting, etc.). So when you read a book (which is a cultural tool) to a child, you help the child come to know more about reading itself or about what the book is about. When you bake with a child you use the recipe book, the kitchen utensils, the oven (all cultural tools) to help the child know more about reading or how to whisk eggs or why you need heat the oven in order to bake anything.

What the more experienced others are doing here is drawing children into their culture and into the meanings of their culture which have been built up over generations. They are inducting children into the particular customs and habits and ideals and values of their culture. In doing this they are enabling the children to become full members of their own cultural groups. This might remind you of the ideas of Rogoff, cited in the first chapter. You will remember that she talked of how children are apprentices to more experienced members of the community and that they learn being alongside these people, watching, listening and joining in. She talked of this as being what she called 'guided participation'.

Vygotsky suggests that in considering mediation we need to think about three concepts which, in translation, are called internalisation, participation and memory. We have thought about memory so let us think about internalisation. We have been talking about how a child, a new learner, when in interaction with an adult who is using cultural tools, becomes able to remember things when those things are no longer present. It is as though the child has internalised or taken into her own consciousness the learning that has taken place. The important point of this is that the child *becomes aware* of what has been learned. Here is an example which so entranced me that I have referred to it many times. It is all about Rehana who is busy exploring the cultures of her home and of her nursery class.

> Four year old Rehana has had four years of being drawn into the culture of her home and six months of being drawn into the culture of her nursery class. She was drawn into the culture of her home by her interactions with her parents and older siblings and inducted into the things that are part of her everyday home life. She understands and speaks Sylheti. She loves the curries and rice her mother serves every day. She knows lots of songs in Bengali. She was drawn into the culture of her nursery class through her interactions with her teacher and her peers: drawn into the things that are part of her weekday nursery environment. She is beginning to speak English and understands it easily. She loves listening to stories with her friends. She is starting to be able to write some words in English. Last week she stayed for school dinner and ate in the classroom with the other children.
>
> Today is her birthday. Her family comes from Bangladesh but she was born in London and has lived there for her whole life. She goes to a nursery in the East End and she is beginning to be able to communicate effectively in both English and Sylheti. For her 4th birthday her mother has said she can have a birthday party and can invite all her cousins and some of her friends from school. From her experience of going to other birthday parties she has requested a birthday cake and her mum has bought one from Marks and Spencer. There are 4 candles on the cake. Rehana is enjoying every moment of this special day. Her mother invited the children from her class to sing happy birthday to her and her cousins have given her a beautiful new sparkly top to wear on this special day. Her friends from school have given her presents too.
>
> (Smidt, 2009, p. 28–9)

Can you see how Rehana is now at the centre of the activity around her birthday? We might describe her as a full and independent member of the culture of English birthdays. How this happened was that she was inducted into this culture when she participated in or witnessed other birthday parties of her peers. This allowed her to remember and internalise the fact that a birthday party requires a cake and candles and that friends need to be invited and that the birthday child looks pretty or smart. She came to be able to do this first through adults drawing her from the periphery into the centre and was then able to sustain her place at the centre by no longer being dependent on adult mediation. But she also internalised her knowledge: this is demonstrated by her knowing what would make her birthday party acceptable to her peers and by knowing what to ask for to make this happen.

It was fascinating to learn from Rehana's mother that for weeks before her birthday party she had been playing birthday parties at home, using her dolls and soft toys as guests, a pretend cake, sticks for candles and parcels she had wrapped as presents. Evidence of memory in action and practice for the real event. Like many children she chose to act out her imagined birthday party, drawing on her own experience of such events and in anticipation of her own looming birthday party.

Practitioners need to:

- be aware of and exploit the *importance of everyday experience*;
- ensure the activities allow for the *diversity of the children's experience to be reflected*;
- ensure that the *resources are matched* to the cultures, customs, languages and interests of all the children;
- ensure there are opportunities for the use of signs and symbols.

Case Study 4 Play in Polynesia

Mary Martini (1994) described the different forms of play of 2- to 5-year-old children playing on the island of 'Ua Pou, Marquesas Islands. The children played unsupervised during the day whilst older siblings were at school. They are described as being able to organise their activities, settle disputes, avoid dangers and negotiate with others. Martini observed that the most common form of play was object play usually involving at the same time doing the same thing and what they were doing included gathering lemons, picking up leaves, sorting and lining up rocks, rolling wheels down to the boat ramp, digging in the dirt, searching for eels and insects, dropping objects from the beach and so on. No negotiating was necessary in this play as the children did the same things together. There are examples of fantasy play where roles are negotiated, rules applied and changed. Martini describes these as including ship play, fishing play, preparing a feast and other things drawn on the lives of the children, where they pretend to do complex things they have observed – launching an outrigger canoe, fixing the motor, fighting off invaders and saving drowning shipmates. Here is the description of what happened during some ship play.

'... Justin and two other leaders pretend to load the ship. Rora plays nearby, washing down the deck. Justin runs up to him and knocks the container of water out of his hands. Rora angrily squats and begins to cry. Justin pats him on the head, gently lifts him to a stand and gives him a can to load on the ship. Rora joins their play.' (p. 96)

The fascinating case study that follows looks at unsupervised play in Polynesia. Martini's analysis is that this shows how key children in the group keep others on track in terms of their social behaviour. For her this example shows how children enable other children to make light of negative events in their play.

Summing up

In this chapter we extended our thinking about memory, looking at memory and experience, memory and role play, memory and semiotics, and memory and cultural tools. In doing this we touched on how babies use their experience, internalise it and then create representations, both complex and abstract. We examined the narratives of role play, how they arise, how children come to choose and play roles, how they negotiate with others, sequence events, invent roles and decide outcomes. In terms of semiotics we examined a number of examples of practitioners using different contexts in order to encourage children to use signs and symbols and systems of symbols in their play. We examined cultural in more detail, again through a number of vignettes.

In terms of the implications for us as practitioners, we reiterated the importance of remembering the role of memory in terms of setting up activities which reflect the experiences of the children and allow them to draw on them and in terms of thinking about how to embed opportunities for using symbolic systems in play. We are also reminded of how we can offer resources to enable children to enhance their play.

Chapter 5

A sense of self

A sense of others

Growing out of using cultural tools and of developing and learning in groups, living in communities and being part of society, young children begin to explore who they are and where they fit in. Much of their exploration for this comes about through their play, which may move from solitary through domestic, into neighbourhood play and school play and beyond to play with rules. In this chapter the focus is initially on the child playing in order to establish who she is and where she sits in relation to her siblings or peers or parents or grandparents or community members. We then move on to look at how children move from private play through to social play as they begin to adopt the roles of others in their world. All of this involves the creation of both roles and rules, and playing with rules is examined.

'No one remains quite what he was when he recognizes himself.'
(Thomas Mann)

Becoming social and aware of self

We know that the human infant is born into a social world and one of the first tasks facing the human infant is to become aware of herself as separate from, but also linked to others. The child gradually gets a sense of herself as a unique individual, living in a community with other unique individuals. For decades, it was thought that a sense of self was slow to develop but the work of Stern (1998) made people think again. He was influential in showing us that it is the very presence of others – willing others – in the lives of human infants that allows them to develop a sense of self-being as part of a social world. Stern argues that the infant soon develops a sense of being with others through regular contact and comes to know about herself as an individual. As the infant encounters things and objects and people and events alongside others, there is a sharing of meaning and the infant begins to get a sense of her own feelings but also those of others. We talk of the infant developing a *theory of mind*, by which we mean developing awareness that other people feel pain, anger, joy and so on. More than that, the implication is that the infant realises that their own feelings can be recognised and shared. Gopnik (2009) tells us that between the ages of 2 and 6 children discover basic facts about how their own minds and the minds of other people work. She calls this 'a causal map of the mind' and what she means by this is how children begin to appreciate the connections, complex as they are, between things like feelings and actions, desires and fears. It is the development of this understanding that leads children to know that people may have different beliefs and values and emotions and these may lead to them behaving differently and have different expectations. She cites a lovely experiment where 14-month-old and 18-month-old babies were offered two bowls of food – Goldfish crackers and broccoli. All the babies loved the crackers and hated the broccoli. Then the experimenter tasted the foods and said 'yuk' to the crackers and 'mmmm' to the broccoli. She then asked the babies to give her some of the food. After some considerable delay the younger babies offered her crackers (we like them, she must too) but the older babies understood that this crazy adult actually liked the broccoli (p. 55).

And here is an example of a very young child showing awareness that something she wanted to look at might be something her doll might also like to look at.

- Annabel (2 years, 2 months) was in the garden with a doll in the push-chair, going up the path. When they stopped to look at the flowers, Hazel (her grandmother) said 'Look at the lovely flowers'. Annabel said 'Dolly like a look at it' and turned the push-chair round so that the doll faced the flowers.

Pat Broadhead (2004) has developed what she calls a *social play continuum* which she suggests can be used to help practitioners observe children at play and analyse what is seen in terms of this. We are not proposing to go into this in any great detail, but some of the things Broadhead tells us are both interesting and relevant. She suggests that through interaction the human infant begins to recognise that actions she makes are responded to by others and this makes it possible for her to not only initiate but also to share, to demand and to reject. The fact that an action the child initiates produces a response means that the child has control over aspects of each interaction. In this way the child can shape her social interactions. Here is an example to illustrate this:

- Jojo throws his toy horse out of the pram. His mother picks it up. He throws it on the floor again. His mother picks it up again. He tries a third time, but this produces a different response. His mum turns to him and says 'Enough, Jojo. I am not your slave!' and although he does not understand the words he understands from the tone that something he has done has produced a different reaction from the previous reaction. He is in the position to determine what will happen next.

We know that infants take note of what the adults do in the home, in the fields, in the crèche or setting. They take note of other children and their play and actions and notice changes in facial expression and hear changes in tones of voice. The child's own behaviour is characterised by facial expression, eye and finger pointing, vocalising, offering things and objects to others or refusing to part with them. These are all communicative and social behaviours.

A startling and highly significant development is the acquisition of language which allows for greater making and sharing of meaning. Now emotional expression flourishes and the child displays self-promoting, but also social behaviours. Two-year-olds are famous for their tantrums. Sadly they are less famous for their ability to empathise, to help, to share, to comfort. But examples of this are relatively easy to find in the literature.

Here are some examples drawn from the work of Anna Freud and Dorothy Burlingham's observations of children brought up together in the Hampstead Nursery during the Second World War.

*   Edith (21 months) had been hurt by Paul (23 months) and cried bitterly. When Sam (20 months) saw Edith unhappy, he came to comfort her …
*   Sophie (20 months) stood in a corner of the nursery and looked at Larry (19 months). Larry noticed her and went to her saying 'Ay! Ay!' Sophie put her arms around Larry. They stayed like that for quite a while (cited in Dunn, 1988, pp. 86–7).

There are many more such examples given in Dunn's book, which is a classic and well worth reading. She talks not only about very young children showing empathy, as in the examples above, but also of children helping one another (as when a 2-year-old expresses concern that his older brother Denny does not yet have a drink) and sharing with one another.

The sort of play we might expect of very young children is probably what is termed *solitary play* – the play where a child interacts with others around playing with objects or things. But Dunn lets us see that *early pretend play* which involves social cooperation takes place much earlier than might have been expected. Here is another example drawn from Dunn. The 18-month-old child, Mary, is involved in a play situation where her older sister Polly has made a birthday cake in the sandpit in the garden. Here is the dialogue:

Polly: Dear Mary! You're three now.
Mary: (nods) Mmm.
Polly: You can go to school now.

Mary: (nods) Mmm ......
Polly: All right then. (Play voice) Hello Mary, I'm Mrs Hunt. Do you want to help me do some of this birthday cake, do you? (Ordinary voice) We'd better do our birthday cake, hadn't we?

(Dunn, pp. 118–19)

At this point Mary appropriately sang 'Happy Birthday' and she and Polly walked around the garden singing. Mary acted the role of baby and behaved as though her big sister were her mother. Dunn notes that Mary was never seen to raise her arms to her big sister other than when she was in the role of baby. She was clearly pretending that her sister was her mother and invoking the rules she had worked out to be appropriate to that relationship.

In our discussions so far we have limited our consideration to children being cared for within the family, but the reality for many, many children is that care goes beyond the family and into the group. In Western societies like ours more and more children are entering daycare settings at a young age and there establishing important relationships with caregivers beyond the family. In developing countries many young children are often cared for by caregivers within and beyond the family – from older siblings to grand-parents or members of the local community. It is important to reiterate that young children construct their own personal, social and cultural identity through their interactions with caregivers and it is through these interactions that they learn to understand their own 'separate nature and their own agency in relation to others and to the inanimate world of objects' (Brooker, 2009, p. 99).

What is it like to be me? What is it like to be somebody else?

Young children working to make sense of their world need to safely explore their position in this world and they do this primarily, but not exclusively through play. In the vignettes that follow try to think about what aspects of their own lives children are exploring through their play. Some observed play reveals things that are distressing about the lives and experiences and feelings of children. You may find some of these case studies disturbing. All are based on personal observation.

• Yehuda's parents have recently separated and he is using the hand puppets to re-create some of the arguments he has overheard.
  He puts the owl puppet on his hand and says, in a deep voice, 'I am sick of the house always being so messy'.
  He puts the cat puppet on his other hand and says in a little voice, 'It's not my fault'.

The owl puppet responds 'I can't find anything in this mess'.
The cat puppet replies 'I tidied it up three times already'.
The owl puppet hits the cat puppet and shouts 'No you didn't! No you didn't!'
The cat puppet starts to cry.

- Maria is 4 years old. She comes into the nursery every day and heads straight for the doll's house and uses the human figures to act out the sexual abuse she experiences at home but putting the 'father' doll on top of the 'baby' doll and making the father doll move up and down. Nothing is said.

- Efimah is a refugee who arrived in the UK in a container, spent time living in a hotel and is now at her fourth school in six months. Every morning she comes into the room, goes to the dressing-up corner and covers herself in a large scarf. Then she sits very still and silent for about ten minutes before taking off the scarf and finding something else to do.

- Harry often comes into the large room of the setting and immediately heads for the wooden blocks where he sets about constructing the tallest tower he can make. He often fetches a chair to stand on to allow him to build a tower that is taller than himself. When he is satisfied with it, he knocks it down, puts the blocks away and moves on to another activity.

It is not difficult to work out what each of these children is exploring in their play. It seems evident that they are trying out, in the safety of play, to re-examine what things feel like. Yehuda is clearly disturbed by the arguments he has overheard and using the puppets he re-creates his version of the arguments and also explores what he feels about violence and sorrow. Maria's play was so disturbing that staff routinely cried when they observed it. Efimah's play is more difficult to analyse but it seems possible that she uses the scarf to isolate herself (as in the container) and then explores the release of removing the cover and emerging into her new real world. Harry has less to confront about himself and his situation in the world. He quite straightforwardly sets himself a challenge to meet.

We have already talked about how children engage in solitary play and social play and how this initially relates to the domestic roles within their experience. You may be familiar with the Western home corner type of role play where children act out the roles of mother, father, baby, brother, sister, grandmother and so on. As children do this they take on aspects and gestures, body language and spoken language of the characters they are pretending to be. You will have seen children who pretend to be mother using the gestures and the tones of voice which they have encountered. In developed countries children are often offered miniature versions of what might be found in the home – miniature tables and chairs and cookers and washing machines; dolls and clothes to fit them; baby cradles and baths and bottles; tool boxes and recipe books and kitchen utensils. These are meant to encourage children to engage in such domestic role play but it is important to remember that what is offered to children is often very mono-cultural. Not all homes are the same and many practitioners seek to ensure that all the children in their group in the setting will encounter things in the home corner that are familiar to them. Here is what Marva, a practitioner in an inner city Children's Centre, said about her provision:

'In my group we have children who come from many different ethnic groups and who need to find at least something familiar to them when they choose to play in the home corner. We try and ensure that the dressing-up clothes are very open-ended; things like sarees and lengths of fabric, different types of hat or head gear, scarves and different kinds of bags. We have kitchen utensils that vary too – chopsticks and plates and bowls and chapatti pans and Turkish coffee pots and baskets in which we keep some of the equipment. We offer newspapers and magazines in the languages and scripts of the children. Sometimes we take the table and chairs into the store room and offer rush mats on the floor.'

(Personal communication)

Children's play moves on from domestic play to community/neighbourhood play (sometimes called functional play). This is where children move on to enacting and exploring the roles of other significant people in their lives as they move from the boundaries of the home to contexts in their immediate environment and community. Many settings will set up areas of the room to suggest and support such play. Examples include markets, shops, clinics, post office, fire station, garage, railway station and so on. In the best practice such areas will be set up in response to an observed interest of one or more children. The roles available to the children expand to include teacher, doctor, nurse, mechanic, boss, worker, shop assistant, secretary, postman, fireman and so on. Observing children engaged in this type of play can be fascinating. Here are some examples based on observation notes made by student teachers:

- Happy and Vincent are playing in the yard. Happy says 'I will be the boss and you can be the man.' Vincent asks 'Am I a good man or a bad man?' 'I am the bad boss. You are the good man, but we are going to bring Superman in to help you when I am bad to you.' 'What are you going to do that's bad?' asks Vincent. 'I am going to take your job away and then you will have no money, no food, no job'.
- Lois is pretending to be the teacher and has arranged the dolls in a circle around her as she leads them in 'circle time'. The tone of voice she uses and the language itself is not that of a small child but very like

the tone of teacher. What is more her gestures and inflections reveal just how much she has remembered and internalised about how the teachers she has encountered behave. 'Right, children' she says, as she claps her hands to get attention. 'No talking now. It is (a long pause) … singing time! Who is going to choose today's song? Let's see who is sitting nicely and putting up their hand'.

- Tanisha and Ubu are both playing in the doctor's surgery. Tanisha is sitting at the table on which are the phone, the appointment book and the pens and pencils. There is a calendar on the wall. Ubu is wearing a white shirt and has a stethoscope round her neck. Averil pretends to knock at the pretend door. Tanisha responds, 'Oh, it's you Mrs Averil. Come in. You are just in time for your appointment. Doctor Ubu, your patient is here.' Ubu takes hold of Averil's hand and says, in a deep voice, 'I think you are really very sick and need a lot of medicine'.

You could probably offer dozens of other examples illustrating just how good young children are at acting the roles of people whose behaviour they have paid attention to and copy. This is an extremely complex set of cognitive tasks and analysing just what is happening here is worth doing. In order to play the role of someone else, the child has to have taken note of just how that person behaves. Does a teacher speak in the same way as mum? Does a doctor act in the same way as mum? The child must not only pay attention to numerous facets of behaviour (the gestures and body language used; the type of language and the tone of voice as well as intonation and expression) but to work out the things that make the behaviour particular. In order to 'become' that person – the teacher or the doctor or the boss, for example – the child cannot simply copy because the child is having to do this in the absence of the physical presence of the person. So memory is involved. And using memory the child then has to construct a script for what might take place when she becomes that person. Where more than one child is involved, things become even more complex because roles have to be assigned or agreed and interactions between the role players somehow worked out. In order for this to happen children have to decide what rules apply.

Rules and play

Vygotsky said that the child is able to engage in pretend play because she is able to begin to separate the visual field (what she sees) from the field of sense, or meaning. This makes play a significant step in the *decontextualisation of meaning*, which is the ability to think about something even when the thing is not present or evident. We have seen how, when a young child explores an object or a thing or a person, she uses perception and this involves examining not only the colour or shape or size or texture of what she is exploring, but also its meaning. It is as though the child asks the question, (implicitly, of course) 'what is this thing?' Vygotsky talks about this as the child being able to separate the visual field (what can be seen) from the field of sense (what can be implied, worked out or guessed at) and sees this as the first step on the road to the development of higher mental functions and of verbal thinking. *This makes explicit the role that play has in cognitive or intellectual development.* For us this is an extremely important statement and one which needs to be understood so that we are able to defend play as being something more than mere fun. Play is an important way of learning.

More than this, it is in play that the ability of the child to take charge of her own activity begins. Any pretend play situation involves a *rule* if we define the word rule as *a specific principle to which the child adjusts*. The child pretending to be the teacher, for example, applies the rules she has worked out from her experience about how teachers speak and act. The child pretending to be a boss speaks and acts in the way in which she has worked out that bosses speak and act. You can see how rules in this sense are not set by someone else but come about through the meaning the child has attached to what has been seen. It is easiest to understand all of this when we think of early pretend play which involves objects or things, although do remember that it applies equally to all aspects of role play. You will remember that we have talked about how young children begin to use one thing to stand for or represent another. The following vignettes illustrate this clearly. The first two involve objects and the third involves playing a role.

- A stick becomes a wand.

The rules the child attributes to wands must then be applied. These rules might say that wands can be waved. They can magic. The child has arrived at these rules through observation, listening to stories, interaction with others and experience.

- A stone becomes a mobile phone.

The rules applying to mobile phones must be applied. They must be held to the ear and one speaks into them or one holds them up in the air and uses them to take a photograph. The child has arrived at these rules through observation, interaction and experience.

- Pretending to be the mother in role play.

The child becomes the mother. The rules of 'being mother' apply. The child must be in charge, or be loving, or be angry in accordance with the mothering the child has experienced and also according to the feelings the child needs to explore. The child has arrived at these rules through observation, interaction and experience.

Vygotsky tells us that what happens in pretend play is a reversal of the initial response to the investigation of objects or things where the object or thing dominates the meaning. The meaning now dominates the object.

The piece of wood *is* a wand and the world *is* now the world of magic; the stone *is* the mobile phone and the child can begin to communicate with others using it; the child *is* the mother and can play out anything in her experience that pleases or concerns her. Here is how Vygotsky expresses this:

> In a critical moment, when for a child a stick is a horse, i.e. when an object (a stick) constitutes a prop for separating the meaning of a horse from a real horse, the fraction becomes reversed and the sense: sense/object becomes predominant.
>
> (Vygotsky 1978, p. 80)

Much of the writing about rules relates to issues around children learning about good and bad, right and wrong. Children learn that there are rules which have to be kept, but they also learn that rules can be made, changed, negotiated and broken. By the age of 5 many children spontaneously invent games with rules. In their pretend play children invent and negotiate rules, change them when necessary and abandon them when they seem no longer necessary.

Let us now return to the small case studies of social pretend play which we looked at earlier in this chapter. This time we are looking at them to try to analyse the rules the children have generated and where these have come from. We are looking at just how complex the thinking and behaviour of each child involved in both the play sequences are. The purpose is to rein-force our awareness of the complexity and power of play as a mode of learning.

- Happy and Vincent are playing in the yard. Happy says 'I will be the boss and you can be the man.' Vincent asks 'Am I a good man or a bad man?' 'I am the bad boss. You are the good man, but we are going to bring Superman in to help you when I am bad to you.' 'What are you going to do that's bad?' asks Vincent. 'I am going to take your job away and then you will have no money, no food, no job'.

Our analysis

Harry and Vincent are playing together and start by negotiating who will play which role – the boss and the worker. The issue of good and bad then emerges as a key theme with the children drawing on experiences at home of overhearing conversations about good and bad, stories they may have heard, things they may have watched on television and so on. The children clearly have a good understanding of why people work, why money is needed and what a bad boss might do. Without knowing more about the home lives of each child it is impossible to be precise, but what we can deduce is that these children live in homes where jobs are precarious and money short. The suggestion of bringing in Superman lightens the tone.

- Lois is pretending to be the teacher and has arranged the dolls in a circle around her as she leads them in 'circle time'. The tone of voice she uses and the language itself is not that of a small child but very like the tone of teacher. What is more her gestures and inflections reveal just how much she has remembered and internalised about how the teachers she has encountered behave. 'Right, children' she says, as she claps her hands to get attention. 'No talking now. It is (a long pause) … singing time! Who is going to choose today's song? Let's see who is sitting nicely and putting up their hand'.

Our analysis

Lois is playing on her own but her play can be described as being social since she chooses to use the dolls to be part of her play. She does not have to negotiate with these participants in her play because they play the silent roles she has allocated them. Nonetheless she has to do some very complex things. She is playing the role of teacher and has chosen the familiar routine of circle time. She knows about this from her experience at nursery. She knows that the children sit in a circle on the floor and that the adult – the teacher in this case – orchestrates what happens. In her chosen role she uses the voice and the actions (slapping her hands to gain attention) she has seen and mimics the type of language she has heard the teacher use at circle time. She insists that the class rules apply (no talking, sitting nicely, putting up your hand) and she even manages the intonation patterns and nuances of the speech of the teacher, evident in her use of a pause used to invite the children to predict what will happen next. Lois is 3 years old. What a lot she has learned!

- Tanisha and Ubu are both playing in the doctor's surgery. Tanisha is sitting at the table on which are the phone, the appointment book and the pens and pencils. There is a calendar on the wall. Ubu is wearing a white shirt and has a stethoscope round her neck. Averil pretends to knock at the pretend door. Tanisha responds 'Oh, it's you Mrs Averil. Come in. You are just in time for your appointment. Doctor Ubu, your patient is here.' Ubu takes hold of Averil's hand and says, in a deep voice, 'I think you are really very sick and need a lot of medicine'.

Our analysis

Three children are involved in this piece of shared pretend play. They are all 4 years old. They have chosen to play in the doctor's surgery set up in a corner of their setting. Tanisha has chosen to play the role of receptionist; Ubu has chosen to be the doctor and Averil is pretending to be the patient. We don't know if the children have discussed the roles they will play but this is unlikely. It is more probable that the children followed one another into the area and then identified possible roles they could play. Each child has worked out what each of their respective roles implies: Tanisha knows that it is her job to welcome the new patient and uses the appropriate vocabulary (appointment, patient) and even addresses her friend Averil as Mrs Averil. She may have worked out a rule that adults (or pretend adults) should be addressed as Mrs or Mr or Ms. Ubu, in the role of doctor, wears a white shirt and a stethoscope and adopts a deep voice, perhaps suggesting the seriousness of the role of doctor. She too uses appropriate vocabulary when she talks of the need for medicine. The three children don't collide in their play. They don't forget what roles they are playing but sustain these until the play sequence ends. This is a tiny fragment of a prolonged play sequence which extended over 45 minutes and was re-started the following day, when Averil was found to be dying!

It is difficult to say, in few and simple words, just how powerful a medium pretend play is for making and sharing meaning. Let us move on to examining another type of pretend play.

Fantasy play, imaginative play

Most children are fortunate enough to have experiences involving their imagination and inviting them into *possible worlds*. They hear stories read and told, listen to the elders telling traditional legends and myths, watch TV or DVDs or games on their computers, go to the cinema or perhaps to the theatre. These experiences take children into new worlds, worlds peopled by characters created by other people. They enter unreal worlds, worlds of the imagination and anything becomes possible. It is not surprising, then, to find children exploring these possible worlds through their play – solitary or collaborative. If you take some time to watch the children at play, you will almost certainly encounter characters and situations unfamiliar to you. You may even hear language that is unfamiliar to you. Here are some examples:

*   Ruby and Abu are playing in the garden. Ruby is rushing around with a stick in her hand, chanting loudly and rhythmically a sequence of sounds. Every so often she stops and waves the stick in the air, touches an object and moves on. Abu follows behind her picking up leaves and sticks and the odd pebble which he puts in a small box he holds in one hand. Jafar comes out and joins in, following Abu and watching what he is doing. 'What are you playing?' he asks. Abu replies, 'She's the witch and we are making spells'. 'I could be the wizard' announces Jafar.

'I am really great at making magic and doing tricks and killing baddies
… and all that. Actually, I could be Batman. That'd be good'. He goes
inside and returns with some string in his hand. 'I need this for making
my magic nets', he announces.

- A group of children are on the outdoor climbing frame and have
  brought out some additional equipment to support their play. They are
  turning the climbing frame into Hogwarts and each child has decided
  to be a character in one of the Harry Potter stories. None of the children
  have read the books but all have seen them on DVD or at the cinema
  and each child is an expert about the stories they are creating. There is
  much discussion about magic powers, the wizarding world versus that
  of the Muggles, the dark arts, Luna and Dumbledore and Sirius Black.
  It is a particular language – one with which each child in this group is
  familiar.
- Hamid and Rashomon are both recent arrivals in the country. Both
  came here with their families from war-torn countries and although they
  do not share a past or a language they seek one another out and tend to
  be together as much as possible. Their key worker noticed them playing
  in the garden with some wooden blocks and an empty plastic barrel.
  Each child was taking a turn to crawl into the barrel whilst the other
  child appeared to be 'on guard' and was heard to shout out something
  which sounded like a warning.

In analysing the first two of these vignettes, we can easily identify some
of the things that have prompted aspects of the play which do not relate to
everyday experience but to the influences which involve books, films, stories and other events relating to what is often called popular culture. In the
first example the children refer directly to Batman, but their play involving
wizardry and the casting of spells relates to many stories and TV programmes
and films. In the second example the play is directly related to the Harry
Potter phenomenon. But it is almost certain that what takes place in the each
play sequence – what the children do and say – relates to their own concerns and preoccupations and interests and fears and experience. In order
to analyse that, we would need more detailed notes made over a longer
period of time.

The last poignant vignette illustrates children working together, but without a shared spoken language, to share their feelings of fear drawn from
each different but related set of experiences.

Exploratory and scientific play

You may remember reading something about the work of Corinne Hutt in
the first chapter. She believed that play and exploration were not the same
and that learning only took place in what she described as exploratory

behaviour. She later changed her ideas to some extent and subsequent theorists have certainly recognised both exploratory behaviour and play as modes of learning. The first months of life of human infants is characterised by the exploration of everything – objects, people, customs, sounds, sights and so on. As practitioners you recognise this in the provision of areas of your setting specifically set up for children to explore – the sand tray, the water tray, the offer of mirrors or magnifying glasses, the planting of seeds, watering of plants, offer of mechanical toys and magnets of collections of things like corks or seeds or sieves or tubes and so on.

A quotation from the ILEA Primary Guidelines, published in 1986, is interesting and reminds us of some of what we have lost through more recent educational initiatives. It states:

> Young children exploring their world are naturally scientific. They use parts of the scientific process spontaneously and unconsciously, as they play with sand and water in the nursery, make paper aeroplanes in the playground, tinker with wind-up toys and many other activities. During their 'play' activities they are building up ideas of what things are like and how they work, by physically trying out their ideas. If something happens that they do not expect they are excited and curious to see if it will happen when they do it again.

Susan Isaacs, in her observation notes on children in the Maltings School, offers some wonderful examples of children's scientific discoveries:

- Phineas (aged nearly four) saw Lena put some sand into a bucket that already had a little water at the bottom. Lena filled it up with sand and then turned it out as a 'pie'. When she turned it out Phineas said 'Where's the water now? It's all sand!' (p. 138).
- Phineas held some wet raffia in the fire, and asked 'Why won't it burn?' Miss C – 'Why won't it?' Phineas – 'Because it's wet'. He held it against the flame for some time and when it began to burn he said 'It's burning now'. Miss C – 'Why is it burning now?' 'Because it's dry'. 'What made it dry, Phineas – 'The flame.'

(p. 141)

Play and gender

Mindy Blaise spent time in an American kindergarten, trying to study what she calls 'gender discourses'. She paid attention to the children at play and engaged in teacher-led activities and listened to their discussion in order to examine what gender roles they assigned to themselves and to one another. Some of her examples are funny; many are troubling. Here is one for you to read.

The children are Anne, Sophie, Alan and Raoul, and she observed them in the role play area where Sophie and Anne were at the stove cooking and talking on the phone, whilst Raoul and Alan were standing on some large wooden blocks and ramps, wearing sunglasses and scarves tied like neckties.

Raoul: Where are you going today?

Alan: I'm going to kill some people. I'm a villain.

Raoul: (Uses a plastic banana as a gun and starts shooting at Alan) Bang, pow, pow, pow! I got you!

Alan: Hey, Raoul … my name is Bond … James Bond (lowering his head toward the floor while looking up with his eyes).

Sophie: Guys … We need a table. (Using a high-pitched and singsong voice. She is standing with her feet apart and with both hands on her hips.

Alan: We can make it later.

Sophie: (Talking into the phone) No, we are eating right now. (Turns to Anne) He's asleep. Someone shot him.

Anne: He said 'I'm afraid.' He has pain. We need to check if the bullet is in his heart.

(Blaise, 2005, p. 2)

A tiny overheard and observed snippet. The children, paired by gender at the start of the observation, at first appear to be following separate play scripts. The little boys are planning to do something 'bad', involving guns and shooting. The girls seem intent on more domestic play. But by the end of this little episode their play has come together. The girls are drawn into the boys' play perhaps because James Bond has been mentioned or perhaps because one of the boys needs help – a role girls often choose to play.

Children not only explore fantasy but aspects of reality that are unfamiliar. On another occasion Blaise overheard two little girls in the kindergarten arguing about who should be mum debating about whether all families had only one mum. Blaise herself intervened assuring the girls that families were different and some families did have two mums. Later she observed one of the girls taking this onboard in their role play. The girls were dressing up for a wedding. Notice how many other difficult areas are touched on in this domestic play.

Theresa: (Walks over to Penny, tapping with her foot.) Where are my shoes?

Penny: (Shrugs, gets up from the black and walks up to Katy, watching her fix a veil on top of her head). Pretend I'm your mom, okay?

Katy: No, no, Theresa's the mother.

Penny: (Lowering her voice while looking down at the floor.) No, pretend there's two moms.

Katy: And I'm the auntie, so I'm getting married ... How about I adopt
          you, how about that?
Penny: Okay. (Turns and walks away)
Katy: Theresa, I adopted Penny ... a long time ago. (Theresa gets up from
          the block and walks towards Katy. Katy ties a scarf around and over
          her veil.) Pretend that Penny's a little girl and I took her.
Theresa: (Nods) Why do you always get to be the bride?
Katy: Because we worked it out .....

(Blaise, p. 168)

Here we have a reference to one of the ploys used by young children to make their play script work – a negotiation about who will do what once the play commences. Think about how difficult it can be, as adults, to negotiate with other people. One of the things involved in successful negotiation is the ability to see things from the point of view of others. In educational jargon this is known as the ability to *decentre*. If you are familiar with the work of Piaget, you will remember that he said that young children could not do this and based his conclusions on an experiment requiring children to sit in front of a model of a mountain and choose a picture showing the view of the mountain that would be seen by characters placed in different positions. Later work showed this to be an inappropriate task and that young children could certainly take on the perspective of other people in situations which made human sense to them. In fantasy play we find clear evidence of children doing this just as we find evidence of them using many other cognitive abilities.

    The most significant implication of all this is the importance of know-
    ing that play is a significant way of learning and to be able to explain
    this to parents and others.
    Another implication is learning how to work out just what skills and
    knowledge all children bring to social and imaginative play.

Play is not what happens after work, to occupy time, or to be pleasurable. It can often be cognitively challenging, requiring the child to use memory, signs and symbols, cultural tools including language, social skills like negotiation and planning and sharing, prediction, and more. You may remember what Vygotsky said in his detailed analysis:

    In play a child is always above his average age, above his daily behav-
    iour; in play it is as though he were a head taller than himself.

(Vygotsky, 1967, p. 16)

Our next case study reminds us of some of the issues we have not yet touched on in this book – the roles of family members and the community in the play and learning of children. In the following example from Albania we read about what one NGO is doing in terms of trying to change national thinking about play and learning. It makes for fascinating reading.

Case Study 5 The Gardens of Mothers and Children Centre

An NGO in Albania has started setting up early childhood care and education centres in a very poor region of Albania where there is poor infrastructure, deep poverty and a paucity of any services for young children. In setting up the centres the NGO has been concerned to consult people in the local communities and to try to involve them in setting them up. In each region an administrative mother was chosen to manage the Garden and its activities and the person selected was chosen by community members and the elderly on the basis of the respect in which she was held and the fact that she had space in her home to set up a centre. The centre is thus accessible to the local community. The Gardens are open to all children from the age of 3 to the age of 6, which is the age at which schooling becomes mandatory. Children and mothers or grandmothers or grandfathers or elder sisters are invited to attend the Garden five mornings per week, and what is entirely new in this for Albania is that the children are not expected to sit quietly and learn by rote but are involved in play and in using water, sand, natural resources, in painting and drawing and games. The administrative mothers and lead mothers were trained by the NGO in how to promote play. Fathers are regarded as being important and each Garden developed its own Board of Fathers – a place for the men to gather and talk about issues related to their roles as father and to what is happening in the Garden. Board members are trained in aspects of child development, non-physical forms of discipline, the importance of fathers in the lives of young children, children's rights and aspects of conflict resolution and mediation.

(Aida Orgocka and Ingrid Jones in *Early Childhood Matters*,
June 2007)

Summing up

In this chapter we have moved on from looking at how children learn that other people have minds, thoughts and feelings and that their feelings and thoughts may all be different. This is an essential step in learning to live in the world as a unique individual but alongside other individuals. We explore how role play enables children to try out the roles of people close to them, then further away from them and ultimately of people imagined and made up. In doing this they have to work out or invent rules, negotiate roles and explore both the physical and the social worlds.

The implications for practice are the importance for us being able to both understand why play, as a mode of learning, is important and to be able to explain this to our colleagues and to parents and carers.

Chapter 6

Sharing feelings and thoughts
Playing at being an artist

This chapter looks at children using both material tools and cultural tools (some of which will also be material tools) in order to share their thoughts and feelings with others. So we look at children playing primarily with sound (music), with movement (dance) and with physical tools (art and design). We are moving into examining how children come to be able to express not only their ideas but also their feelings.

'Educating the mind without educating the heart is no education at all'.
(Aristotle)

Creativity and play

In a nursery class some music is playing and children are dancing to it. One child, in particular, is moving to the music in a particularly sensitive way – her movements being sinuous and complex and highly patterned and directly related to the rhythm of the music. Beside her, another child makes the movements of break-dancing. Later an adult talks to the child about what moved her to dance when she hears that particular music and she says it is because the music makes her want to make fast movements. Later the same adult asks her to talk about some of her paintings that are displayed on the walls of the room. Like her dancing, the paintings are full of movement, with snaking and voluptuous lines, and the dramatic use of space and colour. The child then tells us that her father is a painter. Later in the sequence we see her and some other children sitting at a table on which is a mounted butterfly in a case, together with paper, brushes and watercolours. The child spends a very long time in creating an incredibly beautiful and sensitive painting of the butterfly. The marks the child makes on the paper are clearly drawn from what she sees on the butterfly and show her preoccupation with colour and pattern and sequence and rhythm. The camera, focused on her, shows her looking at the butterfly, and down at her painting; up at the butterfly and down at her painting. It is clear that she is assessing her own work as she paints. Aeryn is clearly a privileged and gifted child.

Note: You can see this video sequence for yourself by going to http:// testsandexams.qca.org.uk/19961.aspx and clicking on the video clip called *Sound and Vision with Aeryn*. The video clips are provided to help those working with children in the English Early Years Foundation Stage assess their progress. There are other video sequences on that same website and some of them are very interesting.

The nursery class or setting attended by Aeryn is clearly one where children's creativity is both promoted and respected. The children's paint-ings on the walls are beautifully displayed and the adults in the room talk to the children seriously about their attempts to share their thoughts and feelings through things like painting and movement.

Defining creativity

Let us start by thinking about what we mean by *creativity*; it is a word often used by those involved in both care and education and integral to the provi-sion in the nurseries in Reggio Emilia. The sense in which the term is used in our provision is to refer to opportunities for young children to paint or draw or write or act or dance or sing or make music. The sense in which it is used in Reggio Emilia is both more complex and more nuanced. In Reggio Emilia creativity and learning are linked; a culture of being prepared to try to do something new and different is fostered and there is rich provision in terms of the physical and cultural tools that will support children's attempts to do this. Rinaldi (2006) talks of learning being a process and when this process is one in which children can use what they need and find in order to come to a new understanding, this is being creative. In short, creativity can be defined as using known elements to make something new and dif-ferent. Piaget talked of children, in play, taking reality in hand in order to own it. Children then *deconstruct* and *reconstruct reality*.

The painter Picasso thought a lot about how creative young children are and tried to analyse what happened to them later in life to destroy this sense of creativity. He is reputed to have said that 'every act of creation is first an act of destruction', and this is very close to Piaget's views and allows us to see that in seeking to make something new and different something old and ordinary may have to be removed, destroyed or altered. When talking about his own work, Picasso said that he began with an idea which then became something else. Watch young children and you will see them do the same thing. Here are some examples that illustrate this point.

- You may remember the 3-year-old playing with a piece of wire which became first a bracelet, then the back of a chair, then a horseman and finally the horse's ear. Something about the malleability of the wire, perhaps, allowed him to see first one thing and then another.

- Ben, as a small child, used a cocktail stick to become a crutch for a small doll, injured during some fantasy play about parachutes; then it became a stick in an umbrella to shield the doll from the sun and eventually he used it as a tool to make a pattern of dots in some dough.
- Oscar, making a picture out of found objects on a large sheet of paper on the floor of his setting placed a tyre centrally on the paper and then scattered pine cones, stones and dried twigs around the tyre. He then sat back to observe what he had made and then, very deliberately, removed everything but the tyre and started again. This time he placed two pine cones within the tyre (for eyes), then a dried twig below the cones (for a nose) and finally made a neat upturned curve out of a row of stones (as a mouth).
- Margot, at dinner time every day, first sorted out all the items on her plate so that one thing did not touch another. Satisfied with that, she then proceeded to make something resembling a human face using the food on her plate. Finally she would eat the food, always starting with the mouth and finishing with the eyes.

Like Picasso, some of these young children begin with an idea which then becomes something else. Quite what Margot is doing is more difficult to work out. Perhaps it helps to know that she is in a Dutch primary school as one of the mainly immigrant children in that particular setting. Food clearly is important in her life and possibly holds some deep symbolic significance for her.

There are some settings and certainly some reception classes that operate a 'plan, do, review' approach or something similar. It is very important to think about what we are saying to children in terms of their ability to make choices and take risks if we operate such systems. Think about whether you believe that by asking children to plan ahead and review back to their original plan you limit their very creativity. After all, if the child changes her plan she may have to justify this to the teacher or the practitioner. In our system, changing one's mind might be seen as an indicator of indecisiveness or lack of commitment. The beauty of the Reggio system is that changing your plan is something expected, valued and celebrated. Similarly, you may want to think very carefully about the effect of telling children what the learning outcomes are for the activities they are involved in. You are, in effect, determining the outcomes for them and nothing could be less creative than this.

 The chief implication is for practitioners to remember that where children learn primarily through play and creativity what they learn cannot be determined in advance.

You will almost certainly be familiar with both *convergent thinking* and *divergent thinking*. Convergent thinking is characterised by repetition.

We repeat what we have seen or heard or learned. Divergent thinking, by contrast, is characterised by a reorganisation of elements. Children seem to find divergent thinking easy, whereas adults often find it difficult, and this may be because divergent thinking requires some loss of control or power because it implies changing one's mind. Another important point emerges here.

In order to promote divergent thinking, which is essential for creativity, we have to build a culture which welcomes individuality in terms of the responses of children.

This individuality does not imply selfishness. It is perfectly possible to have an idea (which is an individual act) but to involve others in carrying it out or responding to it. We need to allow children to be and do something different and to celebrate this without doing so in any competitive sense. So we should seek to build a culture that respects both the individual and the social.

Fashions in education change over time. For many years now creativity has had low priority in education, with strong emphasis being placed on what are sometimes called 'the basics' – literacy, numeracy and so on. More recently it seems that the tide is turning and schools and settings are being urged to 'bring back creativity'. At a recent TED conference Sir Ken Robinson talked about how important it is for those involved with young children to remember that we are thinking about how to equip them to live in a world which is unimaginable to us today. Think about this. Children who start formal schooling in 2009 will be due to retire in the year 2065. Think back 50 years: no mobile phones, no mass access to computers, no Ipods, no game boys or nintendos, no celebrity culture, no endless TV. Perhaps this makes you feel a little nostalgic, perhaps not. Now try to think 50 years into the future. Who can possibly guess what the world will look like then and what skills will be needed in order to live effectively in that world?

Currently the education systems in many Western countries operate on a hierarchy of subjects, going from mathematics and literacy down to creativity, and within creativity art and music have more prominence than dance and drama. Robinson calls this 'education from the waist up', with a curriculum that creates people who live in their heads. Young children do not live in their heads alone. They explore the world through all possible means and are willing to take risks and make mistakes. As we have already seen, being a risk-taker is essential to creativity, but our education system views mistakes as errors and in this way educates children out of creativity. Creativity happens when interaction between disciplines – art, music, design, language, mathematics and so on – is possible. We are back to 'the hundred languages' cited by Malaguzzi.

Time and space for creativity

If the great outdoors is your classroom and your playground, you certainly have space for creativity. Children can run and jump and climb and hide and play alone or in pairs or small groups or large groups. They can explore things on a tiny scale and again on a vast scale. No bells ring; no timetables dictate the order of the day. The children can spend as much uninterrupted time as they need to solve the problems they have identified or express and share their theories and feelings. But the reality for the vast majority of us is very different.

Jerome Bruner spent some of his time visiting the provision for young children in Reggio Emilia and was deeply impressed, like most others who have visited. He spoke of one of the schools he visited as 'a special kind of place, one in which young human beings are invited to grow in mind, in sensibility and in belonging to a broader community' (Bruner, 1998, p. 137). It is significant that Bruner uses the word 'invited', which indicates that the children are not required or expected or coerced into doing anything other than the things they want to do. They clearly have choice and having choice is part of our definition of play. What they are invited to do is to develop in terms of several things:

- First in terms of their abilities to make sense of the world, to raise questions and set about solving these.
- Second in terms of sensibility. This word is little used nowadays and can be defined as being aware of and responsive to things like beauty or colour or sound, or to showing particular awareness of the feelings of others.

So the children in the settings in Reggio Emilia are invited to grow cognitively and creatively and they are invited to do this within the context of a community made up of many people with different values and customs and styles of learning and languages and so on.

There were two things that Bruner regarded as very important in the Reggio Emilia settings – *time* and *space*. Bruner used the words 'mine, thine and ours' when talking about time and space, indicating the importance of taking seriously the needs of all those involved in settings in terms of space and time. Bruner, along with other visitors to the settings in Reggio, noticed how much attention has been paid to the layout of the buildings and the furniture in them and to the way in which the day works. In terms of time, there is no organisation of short periods of time broken up by time indoors or time out, time doing one thing or time doing another. Children choose what to do, with whom, where and for how long. There is no requirement to go to assembly or to do PE, for example. In terms of space, attention is paid to the needs of a community made up of individuals and their interactions.

Malaguzzi talked of the physical environment as a system of *interconnections* and *relationships*. So the rooms lead into one another and are built around a central area which mimics the squares which are found in all Italian towns and are part of the lives of the children. In all the areas there are places where space is almost unlimited, but also small enclosed and secret places. Children choose to use the space to suit their current needs or perhaps are inspired by the spaces to do particular things. But the space has also been planned for adults and it is clear that this becomes a respectful and welcoming environment to learn in, to work in and to visit.

Vecchi (1993), visiting the nurseries, commented on the fact that at the start of the day the children spend much time in small groups and seem to be engaged in planning, discussing and negotiating plans for the morning, or exchanging objects brought from home. Some of the older children appear to select the hidden spaces at the start of the day. Although safety is clearly an issue for all those involved with children, it is not the primary factor in determining space, indoors or out. The space is designed to reflect the culture and the history of each of the settings. Clearly there are similarities and differences between each setting, but the underpinning philosophy means that there are some common features. One of the most well-known of these is the presence in each of the settings of a *studio* or *an atelier*. This is a place for watching an artist at work, for close observation of some of the beautiful things specially collected to be stored in the space, for thinking about what is happening and for having a go yourself.

It was in relation to his impressions of the work in Reggio Emilia that Bruner first used the phrase for which he has become famous and which is the title of one of his books, *Actual Minds, Possible Worlds*. For him the preschool settings were places where children and adults learned together about the real world but also about worlds of the imagination, of fantasy, of narrative – the possible worlds. He said: 'It (the setting) must be a place where the young discover the uses of the mind, of imagination, of materials, and learn the power of coding these things together' (p. 137).

All children will benefit from having access to things which will support and enhance their experiences. These may be physical or natural or found or made things, they may be cultural tools but all will be mediated by those who are more expert in whatever area the child is considering.

Objects, materials and cultural tools to support play and creativity

Many settings in the developed world are extremely privileged in terms of the wealth of resources available to children and their educators and carers. Reggio Emilia is a supreme example of privilege beyond the reach of most, but we can still learn things from their underlying philosophy of respect and relationships. We have talked about the central meeting area – the piazza – and seen how this, for the children in the Reggio preschools and settings, relates to their out-of-setting experience. Squares are a feature of the daily lives of the children and their families and communities, and having a central meeting area is something they are familiar with and which allows them to draw on their prior experiences of meeting friends, running around, watching people, joining in, standing back, collaborating, talking, listening and a host of other social and physical skills. It is interesting to think about what such a piazza means in settings which claim to be based on the Reggio Emilia model. But it is perfectly possible to think about what features of life outside of the setting can usefully be replicated in the setting.

In the Reggio Emilia settings the use of space is taken a step further by the introduction of a place where children have the chance to see creative people at work and this is an interesting idea and one which genuinely sees play as a cultural form of learning. If, as Noschis, the Swiss architect says, play is something that should not 'isolate children from the neighbourhood but only be a privileged space for playing what is observed in the neighbourhood' (Noschis, 1992, p. 7), offering children opportunities to see people at work extends both their neighbourhood or community and their experience. You may recall that when we talked in a previous chapter about role play we saw how children move on from domestic play to neighbourhood play where they explore the roles and rules governing the worlds of the doctor, the teacher, the nurse, the shop keeper, the bus driver and so on. If we offer them opportunities to see people making things, creating things and solving problems relating to how to express both feelings and ideas, we further extend their experience and opportunities. As we have already seen in most of the settings, there is a studio or an atelier. In this space, there are collections of materials for making things and representing feelings and ideas. These include mark-making materials like pens and pencils and brushes; surfaces to make marks on; equipment for three-dimensional work, including clay and clay tools, wood and tools for woodwork or carpentry; materials for making large and small models; light tables and more. In addition there are things to look at and feel to inspire children's urge to express themselves. These range from large things like tree trunks or intricate bits of machinery to tiny objects. Then there are aids to understanding more about what you see – mirrors and magnifying glasses and transparent papers and so on. And there are collections of beautiful things – buttons, marbles, bits of glass, stones and pebbles, dried plants, string and rope and wire and wool, fabric and ribbon and lace – anything and everything, all displayed so that the children can see them and explore them. Now collections are possible for all of us – whatever our circumstances. Children are great collectors and will build up collections of corks or bottle tops or old paper clips or pine cones or shells or leaves. And collections can be very useful in mathematical, technological and scientific thinking.

None of that should sound unfamiliar to you, although the scale on which these things are offered is huge and very probably far beyond anything you could manage in your setting. But the principle still applies. Most interesting is the presence of someone working in the atelier. The person could be a sculptor or a painter or a carpenter or dressmaker – someone making something to express their ideas and feelings. The person is there as a model of someone working creatively and someone to whom the children can talk and turn to for suggestions, help, support or advice.

 The implications for practice are very clear: ensure that children have ongoing and easy access to all that they need for drawing and painting, making models, handling interesting and unusual and beautiful things or using what is to hand in order to address their needs and concerns and allow them to raise and answer questions.

Be careful not to interpret this as a shopping list. Rather, see it as finding ways of allowing children to use what is to hand in order to make what they choose.

Here are some examples, relating to children playing at home or in settings.

- The first relates to a 4-year-old at home, who spotted an empty Panadol packet (Panadol being an analgesic). The packet was blue with blue and white printing on it and inside were two plastic sheets in which individual tablets had been sealed. The little girl got up from her chair at the breakfast table, fetched a pair of scissors and started to cut out the individual indentions from the plastic sheet. Then she cut round the edges of the blue packet and folded it out so it became a large square piece of soft card. Then she cut around one end of the square card to produce what emerged later as a head. She went upstairs to fetch a role of sticky tape with which she set about taping the cut out bubbles onto the cardboard square. What finally emerged was a policeman wearing a blue uniform, studded with buttons. All this was done without talk, intervention or interaction, but clearly with a purpose and a deep sense of design (drawn from Kress, 1997, p. 34).
- A theatre group in the Eastern Cape in South Africa were keen to take their theatrical production into an early years setting. They adapted a traditional folk tale about a frog and the river and used dried stalks of corn as props. The children were totally engrossed in the story and afterwards came over and felt the corn stalks and looked at the minimal props that had been used – lengths of fabric, corrugated card and old tin containers and bits of wood and said they wanted to 'make' their own story and their own props. The staff were delighted but said each child had to bring one thing to the setting next day – one thing that could be

turned into something else. They insisted that nobody was to ask their carers to 'buy' something. The next day the children came in with a fantastic collection of dried seed pods, sticks, stones, old tobacco tins, lengths of wire, buttons, bits of netting and sacking, shiny threads of ribbon and more. (Personal observation, 2009)

A clear implication arising from this is for practitioners to place emphasis on children learning through their engagement with others – children and adults – and in particular with those who are 'experts' at something.

Although few of us would be able to afford to employ full-time artists or craftspeople in our settings, we could certainly make enquiries about what artists or musicians or groups might be willing to come into our settings and model what they do for the children. This would clearly not be as effective as having a permanent atelier with an artist on site, but it would provide the children with models of real people doing real expressive things in front of them.

Here are some examples:

- Kath, the mother of two children in the primary school, was asked to come in and set up her easel in the hall so that the children, passing through, could watch her paint. In the days that followed easels were set up in the hall and children were allowed to go and paint at any time during the day.
- Students on an art course at a local college were asked if they would set up an installation in the playground for the children to observe and play on. The students were interested in doing this and some of them used it as the basis for their assessed work. The children were able to watch them setting up the installation (made of tyres and ropes and netting and wooden panels). Although they had not planned to do this, the students invited the children to help them paint the completed piece and the children then got involved in designing their own pieces of playground equipment.
- A well-known weaver in the local community was invited to set up her loom in the nursery and demonstrate weaving to the children. The children showed enormous interest and many of them stood for long periods of time watching the threads and the growing pattern of the emerging weaving. After the completion of the work the head of the nursery bought three small looms which became permanent features of the nursery.
- Young musicians from a borough music service were asked if they would come and play some music for the children in the nursery class. The musicians (aged from 10 to 17) brought in percussion instruments,

string instruments, brass and woodwind and played a selection of music – classical, folk and pop to the children. At the end of the performance individual children were invited to come up and have a go at playing an instrument of their choice.

Playing with music

Very recently the educators in Reggio Emilia have made links with educators from across the world in Venezuela. There, as you may know, a national system for introducing all children to classical music has been in place for more than three decades. In 1975, an amateur Venezuelan musician, José Antonio Abreu, founded what was called 'Social Action for Music' and became its director. The goal of the scheme was to use an orchestra as a model for an ideal society and to involve children from all over the country, and particularly from the most impoverished regions, to participate. Children were given musical instruments to play. Initially the children were given classical stringed instruments such as violins or cellos, but the range of instrument was later broadened.

All the children were expected to practise daily and to join in with local musical events on a regular basis. The model was supported by different administrations, culminating in that of the current government of Hugo Chavez who is a dedicated and committed supporter. This experiment is a wonderful example of using something creative – in this case music – to work towards social change. The children who, without the programme, would have had limited educational experiences and options, end up now being part of a group which is celebrated publicly by others in the community and more widely. Music requires a strict discipline. An orchestra cannot play unless each member respects each other member. It is an example of a functioning collaborative approach which would not work without cooperation and negotiation. This system, known as *El Sistema*, has been widely recognised and internally successful. Abreu, its founder, was appointed as Special Ambassador for the development of a Global Network of Youth and Children orchestras and choirs by UNESCO in 1995, and also as special representative for the development of a network of orchestras within the framework of UNESCO's 'World Movement of Youth and Children Orchestras and Choirs'. At the time of writing, it is believed that there are over 100 youth orchestras and 55 children's orchestras (numbering more than 100,000 young people in total). Supported by the government, El Sistema has started to introduce its music programme into the public school curriculum, aiming to be in every school and to support 500,000 children by 2015. The programme is certainly expensive to run, but the government has recognised that the quality of life of the children involved improved so dramatically as to significantly reduce their involvement in crime and drugs. Other countries across the world, seeing the success of the programme, have started to try to replicate it (just as the Reggio model has been copied), but it is not certain that initiatives like this can easily be replicated.

Like El Sistema, the whole Reggio Emilia model has now become famous and vast and more and more of a business. Yet the concepts on which both were built are relevant and interesting to many educators: in one the philosophy of a pedagogy built on relationships, in the other using a collaborative creative enterprise to effect social change.

Practitioners must consider seriously how to make music available to all children in order for them to express their feelings. In doing this, they should think about opportunities for children to listen to and make music alone or in groups; the provision of instruments bought or made; the presence of manuscript paper and song books to encourage children to invent and record music; opportunities for collaboration, and visits from musicians and music groups.

In El Sistema, collaboration is essential for the orchestra or band to operate at all. Even if you have only five people playing musical instruments, unless they conform to certain rules (playing in the right place, on the right note, for example) instead of music there would be chaos. Multiply that by five and the chaos becomes unimaginable. No one is suggesting that we require children to conform as an orchestra or band must, but thinking about how to help children become more collaborative, more sensitive to the needs of others, more able to negotiate, communicate, share and take turns is important.

The case study that closes this chapter is a brief account of the early years curriculum developed some year ago in New Zealand. For many, this experiment in terms of providing opportunities for all young children explicitly celebrating diverse cultures, ways of rearing children, languages and relationships offers much to learn from.

Case Study 6 Te Whariki

New Zealand's early years curriculum, Te Whariki, was developed many years ago in 1998 and applies to all settings which are registered or chartered. It is admired by many, primarily because it was designed to be really inclusive of New Zealand's children and took account of the views of parents and community leaders in its development. It is not subject-based but made up of four strands with goals attached and the strands are woven together with the four underlying principles in a similar fashion to the traditional woven mat of the Maori people – the whariki, hence the name. The four strands are: Whakanana – empowering children to learn and grow; Kotahitanga – encouraging children to learn and grow holistically; Whanau tangaga – including the wider world of family and community as an integral part of children's learning; and Nga hononga – learning through responsive and reciprocal relationships with people, places and things. The links with the approach of Reggio Emilia in terms of the emphasis on empowerment, holistic learning and a pedagogy based on relationships are clear and you can see how well play, as a mode of learning, would work in such a curriculum.

Summing up

In this chapter we have effectively looked at the child playing at being an artist of some sort. We are not suggesting that the child has set out to behave like a painter or sculptor or musician or dancer, but rather that the child, equipped with some ideas or feelings to explore and encounter the materials to allow her to do this, draws on what experience she has of seeing expert others at work. We have drawn on case studies from Italy and Argentina in this chapter and in the next chapter we continue to look at the notion of 'playing at' to look at the child as symbol user.

The implications for practice are many. We need to move away from predetermined goals to allow children to follow their own interests and passions. We need to value divergent thinking and welcome individuality in the responses of our learners. We need to do the best we can to make the space usable for creative work and to organise the day into chunks of uninterrupted time. We could certainly consider inviting experts into our settings to demonstrate what they are expert at to the children so that they have models of creative adults. We need to make the arts – drawing, painting, singing, dancing, making music – making things integral to the curriculum and we need to think about what opportunities we provide for collaborative play. There is much, indeed, to think about here.

Chapter 7

Sharing feelings and thoughts

Playing at being a symbol user

In this chapter we continue to explore what children do in their play as they find ways to share their thoughts and ideas and feelings with others, but now through the symbolic systems available to them – letters, words, numerals, symbols and signs. So we examine how children begin to use symbolic systems, invent and use rules relating to these and play the roles of reader, writer, audience, composer, scribe and explorer.

'Fill your paper with the breathings of your heart.'

(William Wordsworth)

To begin at the beginning ...

Zac has an older brother and sister, both of whom use email. He was very excited to get his own email address and immediately emailed his grandmother to let her know. Here are some extracts from their brief communication, included precisely so that you can admire the rules of written English that Zac is inventing:

i got your mesj. it is raning love Zac

You are very good at emailing. Have you got a nice umbrella to keep you dry when it rains?

Sandra

yes Sandra but if it is raining the socu is cansd

love zac

Hi sandra thank you for remd me a bat emails. I am going to kis land nes wik. love zac.

Note: Since I know little about the geography of Australia, I needed to get the help of Zac's older sister in decoding this. You may well have worked out that the family is going to Queensland next week.

Zac is already at school and is learning the conventions of English writing and spelling. But this is not school and so he feels free to send a message as well as he can using whatever rules he has worked out or learned. And you will have no difficulty in understanding what he says: his rules are so sound. For example, his spelling of the words 'soccer', 'cancelled' and 'reminding' are both logical and immediately recognisable. Much has been written about how young children come to use letters and letter-like shapes to communicate their thoughts and ideas to others. There is not enough space here to go into this in great detail: what is offered is an overview of how hard children work at 'being writers'.

Much of the evidence comes from the writing children do at home (like Zac) and this is probably because at school or in the setting there are more constraints on what the child is expected to do. Many children are asked to do inappropriate things in formal settings (under the umbrella of the national strategies), whereas at home they are free to really play and explore their rapidly expanding understanding of what symbols represent and how they can be used.

All children, wherever they live, need to learn to become users of symbols if they are to become literate and numerate. Many children encounter writing events in their everyday lives. In some highly literate and visual societies children encounter such events in a huge range of contexts and situations. Jennie twitters online. Sukvinder sends an email. Junior leaves a message for mum on the notice board. Eva marks off the days till the concert on the calendar. The census form drops through the mailbox and needs to be filled in. Umut's dad reads the newspaper. Abdullah chants the Koran in the mosque. The traffic warden writes a parking ticket. The doctor writes a prescription. Paballos' teacher writes on the blackboard. Children try to make sense of all this – and they do so by watching, looking for patterns, trying to find the rules and by playing at writing and at reading and at counting for themselves. As they play they may include writing in their play. And as they do this they start to reveal the assumptions they are making about how writing works. They may notice that if you write with your finger on the window pane, the mark you make disappears – but if you make a similar mark with a pen on the wall, it doesn't. They may also notice that nobody seems to mind much if you write with your finger on the window pane, but you get a very different response if you write with pen on the wall! They may notice that some of the marks they make look like something real, something recognisable: others look like squiggles. As they experiment they begin to distinguish between marks that might represent real things – which they call pictures – and marks which stand for things – which they call writing.

We could make a shopping list by drawing pictures of all the things we are going to buy but we don't do that. It is too time-consuming. We find a shorthand – a simpler way of recording. We write words which, like pictures, represent the items. They are symbols. We write for many reasons and children start to work out all the possible reasons for writing and the possible audiences to read what is written. Baghban (1984) wrote a case study charting the development of her daughter Giti, from her first attempts at writing to being a confident 'writer' at the age of 3. Giti grew up in a literate family and started to incorporate mark-making into her play from very early on. By the age of 17 months she preferred to write with a ballpoint pen or a felt-tipped pen to writing with a crayon. Her mother, intrigued by this, suggested that the expert models of writing Giti found around her, such as her mother and her grandmother, never chose to write with crayons. By the age of 25 months she was including some of the letters of her own name in her strings of writing. As her discoveries about the world of writing developed, she showed that she understood that English writing goes from left to right and from top to bottom. She understood that some letters tend to be repeated, some things get underlined and that print carries meaning and can be used for different purposes.

Ferreiro and Teberosky (1979) studied groups of preschool children in South America and found that these very young children had developed some hypotheses about writing. These included the following:

1　The written form of something must relate in some way to the object it stood for or symbolised. So they assumed that the word for 'elephant' would be very long and the word for 'mouse' very short.
2　For something to be a word it needed to consist of at least three letters and that all three letters need to be different.

Before the imposition of the literacy strategy on schoolchildren in England, much attention was paid to emergent writing, the processes children go through as they work out just what writing is, how it is done, what and who it is for. The term makes clear that children, when trying to make sense of writing, behave just as they do when they are trying to make sense of spoken language or of the physical world or of the feelings of others. Through the processes of (a) abstracting, (b) hypothesising, (c) constructing, and (d) revising, children come to understand the rules of the world. Let's look at each of these in some detail to see how they apply to writing.

• *Abstracting* means trying to work out or extract the essential feature, or pattern that gives us the rule. Young children, as they acquire their own language, spend a long time listening, watching and sorting things out. An example of a rule they have abstracted is the assumption that all verbs in the past tense, in English, add 'ed'. This leads to the familiar errors 'I goed' or 'The birds flied' – forms of spoken English that no child would have heard from a fluent adult speaker of the language.

In terms of writing, one of the rules very young children extract is the example of the minimum number of letters it takes to make a word, cited above.

- *Hypothesising* means thinking about 'what if' or 'how' – a search for an explanation. We see evidence of this in children's exploratory play, when they encounter something new and spend a considerable amount of time exploring the new thing through all means available. In terms of writing, the child selectively imitates aspects of writing behaviour they have observed and been interested in. So Gita chose to use a ballpoint pen rather than a crayon when writing – imitating the adults around her and their writing behaviour.

- *Constructing* involves the child in addressing the question 'What can I do with it?' and here the child, imitating expert behaviour, focuses on particular aspects of this behaviour. The young child in the home corner who acts out the sequences familiar from home is putting together her acquired skills and knowledge and trying them out 'like an adult'. Revising happens all the time, in all aspects of learning. As adults respond to the babble of small babies, the babies refine and modify the sounds they produce so that they become closer and closer to the sounds of 'real words'. With writing, as children make marks which become close to recognisable letters, the response of supportive adults encourages the child to repeat these symbols intentionally. We are back to one of the key features of the role of adults with regard to play – that of sharing the child's focus of attention.

 We need to:

- set up opportunities, contexts and resources to inspire children to write;
- ensure that children have easy access to materials with which to make marks (chalk, pens and pencils and markers and brushes and so on) and materials to make marks on (blackboards, different types and sizes of paper, lined paper and blank paper, envelopes, card) and to computer keyboards;
- take seriously the attempts at writing children make and not ignore or dismiss them because they are not 'correct'. So when a child presents you with what appears to be random scribble, it is important to examine this carefully to try and see what it is the child is drawing on and what the child is trying to do. We urge you not to ask 'What does this say?' because it may not be communicative in intention but just an exploration of letter-like shapes, or using the space on the page;
- consider what models of the process and of the products of writing we make available. Children should see us writing and should also have a

wide range of examples of different types of writing. So in addition to books we might think of offering alphabet posters (of the scripts of the languages spoken by the children); magazines and comics; songbooks and poems; recipe books, phone books, maps, guides and, of course, printed materials in the languages of the children in your group. All of this will help children appreciate the fact that we write for different audiences and for different purposes.

Towards the 'tune on the page'

We need to keep in mind the importance of children exploring signs and symbols within the context of their social and cultural lives. Where a child encounters adults who are interested in what she is doing, who treat her as an equal partner in any exchange and who recognise and value the cultural and linguistic input the child brings from home, this 'active, thinking, hypothesising child' (Whitehead, 1990) can try out her developing ideas about writing through play. It is important to remember that writing involves at least three sets of distinct activities and the skills involved in these. There are the skills of *transcription* – what you need to do physically to make the marks on paper. There is what is involved in *acquiring the rules of written language* – things like how words are spelled, that sentences end with full stops and that a question ends with a question mark, for example. And there is the skill of *composition* – deciding what to say and how to say it. This is 'the tune on the page'. If we allow children to explore writing through play, we find that they explore all of these aspects of written language.

The earliest thing that children explore is what they need to do physically in order to make marks on paper. Even at the age of 2 or 3 years young children demonstrate that they will use different physical movements for writing from those they use for drawing. Karmiloff-Smith (1994) observed that very young children, asked to mimic drawing, used large movements, keeping the crayon close to the paper. When asked to 'write' they tended to make smaller marks and lift the tool from the paper.

As children start to explore the conventions of writing marks which represent writing, they start to explore the arrangement of the letter shapes on the paper. Very early writing appears to cover the page randomly, sometimes going from left to right, sometimes from top to bottom, sometimes around the edges of the paper. Remember that the rules regarding the direction in which print should go will vary from language to language. Not all languages go from left to right and from top to bottom of the page (see Figure 7.1).

Children also play with purpose and audience. Ben wrote 'a shopping list' and later allowed his grandmother to put what he called 'proper' writing next to his invented symbols (see Figure 7.2).

Figure 7.1 Themba said that this was writing and not drawing.

Abiola found an envelope and put some marks on this, telling her mum that it had to be posted. She has used many intricate letter-like symbols and her writing went from left to right, top to bottom and resembles the way in which an envelope might be addressed (see Figure 7.3).

 It is important for us to know which languages the children are familiar with so that we can understand their early attempts at writing. We need to familiarise ourselves with what the scripts used by the families in our settings look like so that we can interpret accurately and sensitively what the children are doing as they make marks.

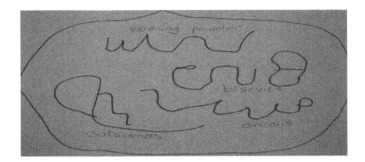

Figure 7.2 Ben's shopping list.

Figure 7.3 Abiola's envelope.

Just for fun: starting to work out the rules of written language

The scripts of the world's languages are extremely varied and you can get an indication of just how many languages, scripts, rules, variations, styles and features there are if you go to www.geocities.com/Athens/Academcy/9594/. We looked at the Tibetan written language (the examples below come from this website) and found it beautiful and quite unfamiliar (see Figure 7.4). It seems to share no features with English or with other European languages which share a common script. When you look at the few examples below, you begin to understand something about the difficulties facing the many, many children who come here with languages other than English and try to utilise the features of one or other or both or all of their languages. You might want to remember that there are more children in the world who speak more than one language than those who speak just one.

Traditional Losar Greeting

Figure 7.4

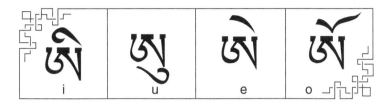

Figure 7.5 The names of the vowels are – gi-gu, shup-ju, dreng-bu and na-ro.

Figure 7.5 shows the vowels or *dbyangs* (yang). Each letter below has an inherent 'a' pronounced like 'but'. In order to change this vowel to another sound (i.e. if the vowel is not 'a'), a mark is placed above or below the consonant. A vowel written alone uses either the Tibetan letter *a* or *'a* – the difference in transcription symbol is only to represent a different letter form. *I* is pronounced like 'fit'. *E* is pronounced like 'May'. *U* is pronounced like 'food'.

Figure 7.6 shows the numerals.

Figure 7.6 1 - ga; 2 - gwa; 3 - gya; 4 - gra; 5 - gha; 6 - gla; 7 - rga; 8 - lga; 9 - sga; 10 - grwa; 11 - rgwa; 12 - rgya; 13 - sgya; 14 - sgra.

Playing at writing

As children play at writing, they begin to show what they have already worked out about writing. Remember what Vygotsky said about children in imaginative play standing a head taller than themselves? It seems that in playing at writing children also stand a head taller than themselves. Analysing what they do shows just what they already know. In the following example 4-year-old Kirsty explained that she had written 'Baa baa black sheep' (see Figure 7.7). Her teacher noted 'Kirsty knows that writing can convey a message; that it goes across the page in lines and it is different from drawing. I think she has drawn on her experience of looking at newspapers or comics'.

Figure 7.7 Kirsty writes Baa Baa Black Sheep.

Children also begin to explore the rules of our spelling system. English is not a phonetic language and children struggle to work out the rules of how the sound system relates to the symbolic written system. Research shows that when young children first start to write in order to communicate, they often use the name of a letter to stand for a word or a syllable. Glenda Bissex (1980) wrote a book based on her analysis of how her son, Paul, became a writer. The book itself is easy and delightful to read. Paul, at the age of 5 wrote this message: RUDF. Can you guess what this means? Are (R) you (U) deaf (DF)? A mere six months later Paul wrote this: WN U ST I GT SD. It says 'When (WN) you (U) shout (ST) I (I) get (GT) sad (SD)'. In a short space of time Paul has elaborated his earlier hypotheses about writing. He had spaces between the words and was beginning to use the initial and the last sound of words, combined with letter names, to convey meaning. At 6, Paul was writing things like this: WEN YOU GO FISHING YOU NED A FLOT. This is sufficiently close to conventional spellings for it to be easy to decode. Paul has learned to recognise and write some useful words like 'you' and 'go'; he asked for help with the word 'fishing' and used the rules of spelling he had generated to write the remaining words. By the time Paul left the Infant School, he had little trouble writing perfectly comprehensible pieces.

But there is more to writing than transcription, grammar and spelling. Writing is, crucially, about communicating. What you say matters. The famous writer on reading Frank Smith (1982) drew a distinction between transcription and composition, explaining that transcription refers to the 'secretarial' aspects of writing – things like spelling, punctuation, formation of letters, orientation on the page and so on. Composition refers to what is written – it relates to the creative side of writing. Writing then offers children the opportunity to create worlds, people them, write for an audience and express their ideas in many ways. The links to imaginative and fantasy play are clear. Myra Barrs (1991) (who invented the phrase 'the tune on the page') describes written language as being 'stored in the ear'. We experience the characteristic rhythmic structure of texts or genres through their intonational patterning, and when we write we draw on the store of tunes we know and on our sense of how such tunes are made. Part of learning to write is therefore a question of learning how to write the tune, and of learning what resources there are at our disposal to enable us to create tunes for our readers. *What* children write is at least as important as *how* they write it.

 Many implications from all of this including the following:

- Helping children develop a store of tunes in their heads by reading aloud to them and singing to them and telling them stories and poems and chants. They need to hear a range of voices and patterns of intonation so that they can use these when they need to. The greater children's exposure to these, the more material they have to draw on when composing for themselves.
- Inviting children to make up their own stories and record these for them and make them into books. We can involve parents and carers in this.

Here is a vignette to illustrate this:

At an inner London primary school they have a regular book-making session which is open to children and to their parents. The parents of the youngest children come along to the sessions and make books for their children. These are often simple stories, simply illustrated and written in the first language of the author. Sometimes the books are then made available in another language and in English (see Figure 7.8 and Figure 7.9).

- Creating contexts to inspire different reasons for writing. There are many examples in the literature, particularly the work of Nigel Hall.

Here is a vignette to illustrate this.

Babette told the children the story of Jack and the Beanstalk and overnight she wrote a letter on a very large sheet of paper and in very large print. The letter was addressed to the children and was from the giant, telling the children that he was very lonely and nobody loved him and he just wanted to have a friend to make him happy. She provided lots of writing paper and envelopes and cards and a letter box and the children engaged in a furious bout of letter-writing to the giant. All of them wanted to be his friend and they invited him to tea, to their class, to sleepovers, to come and play on their Wii and so on. Here are some of their letters, invented spellings and all:

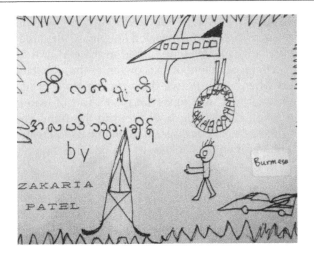

Figure 7.8 This book was written in Burmese by a mother for her young son. It tells of a trip home.

Figure 7.9 This more elaborate book was written and illustrated by the mother of Sophie and Phoebe and based on the Meg and Mog books.

DR JINT U CN B MI FREND

I WL MK U A JINT CUP OF T

CUM TO MI HOUS AND MI MUM WL GIV U A HUG

Children find out about writing through their play and through their interactions. They move from what they understand, getting closer and closer to conventional forms and, in doing this, are able to work out the rules of these conventions. Margaret Meek (1991) insists that they do this by persisting, reflecting, learning, correcting, ordering and refining not only their writing (or spelling), but also their thinking. Bissex (1980) tells us that when we think of children's development in writing, we are thinking about how well children repeat those forms of writing selected and refined by our culture. It may be that we think of our writing system as a given, and think of children as developing towards this. Yet the truth is that when we look back over time we see the writing system itself evolving and developing and it seems that the child's literacy learning is cut from the same cloth as our written language development.

Numbers too

Many young children are fascinated by numbers – what they stand for, how they can be used and how they operate. Here are the examples of two children for whom numbers are mesmerising.

- Ben recently asked how the London buses got their numbers and wondered whether route 1 meant that it was the first bus to be numbered or that it was the shortest route. No one knew the answer to that question.
- Door numbers were very significant to Dominic and that led to an interest in odd and even numbers. (You can read more about Dominic and his passion later in this section.)

In their play children often use numerals or numbers, real and invented. There is an example cited in Worthington and Carruthers (2003) of a child in a reception class who chose to draw a picture of her younger sister. On this picture she wrote a recognisable numeral 2 and then tried to solve the problem of making her picture show that her sister was actually not 2 years old but 2 and a half years old. Her solution was to draw something that looked like half of the numeral 2. In this example we see a child brilliantly using her growing understanding of rules to apply them to symbols.

Hilary Faust (2010) reminds us that it is important for those working with young children to understand just how much children have to understand in order to deal with and use numbers and numerals. She uses the example of the number 3 and considers the different meanings that can be attributed to just that one numeral in the everyday experience of children. They may know the story of the three (3) little pigs. They may have seen the number 3 at the front of a bus. They may have seen page 3 in a book. Three (3) means something different in each of these. The first statement relates to a cardinal number that is a set or group of things (father bear, mother bear and baby bear); in the second statement the number is used as a name or a label, telling people what route that particular bus follows; in the third statement the number is used as an ordinal number being about the order of pages in the book, 3 being between 2 and 4. Faust tells us that:

> All of this matters because it gives us insight into the complexity of understanding about number for the young child, who has to work out which meaning applies. Haylock and Cockburn (1989) point out that: 'at a very early age the child encounters one enormous difficulty that runs right through mathematics: that one symbol is used to represent vastly different situations' (p. 23). Often children will be focused on one meaning, as we can see in the example of the four-year old who was baking cakes with his mother. She asked him how many of the six cakes would be left if they ate four, and he replied 'five and six', much to her surprise. It seems he was attending to ordinal number, when the expected response involves cardinal number (take four away from a set of six cakes, leaving two)
>
> (Faust, 2010, pp. 112–13)

Here is a case study submitted by Hazel Abel, who has studied and worked with young children. She became aware of her grandson Dominic's passion for numbers very early in her life. I asked her to write something for this book about this and it is included here.

House numbers

Every time Dominic comes to stay, we have to go into the block of flats at the corner of the street to see the numbers on the front doors in sequence: up one flight of stairs and then along to each flat to see the numbers and so on. Then he discovered there were more blocks of flats nearby so these were investigated in the same way. He doesn't live in London and there are no flats near his home. We also have to go all the way up to the end of the street to see the numbers on the front doors. Once he noticed that a number had nearly fallen off and was lying on its side. He laughed and laughed.

He has found a cul-de-sac street near his home which goes in a circle at the end so you don't have to cross the road to count all the numbers.

Dominic noticed numbers outside block of flats written 1–5 and asked why they didn't write all the numbers. His mum explained.

Dominic takes control of counting

Dominic had a basket of cutlery and laid them out on grass in a long line. Then I suggested he could put all the spoons in a line and so on and he then counted them and took some away from the group, saying how many were left. I thought he might have been doing something similar at his nursery so I asked 'How many will you need to make it 10?' but he wanted to take over, 'No, I am going to make it 11,' which he did, then he put another one on and said '12, now I got.' He carried on doing this, reaching 27, and then he noticed that I was writing. 'What are you doing?' he asked. I told him I was writing down what he said and did. I showed him what I had written. Then he started to get really interested and involved; 'You haven't written all the numbers. You keep forgetting lots of numbers.' His mum explained that it was like the notice outside a block of flats saying 'nos. 1–5' and that you can use a dash to mean all the numbers in between.

Dominic was fascinated and we started a sequence, he counted, I wrote. First he counted from 58 to 67 and I wrote 58–67. Dominic checked that I had got it correct. We kept going and the interesting thing was that his counting was incorrect; he is not a conserver and didn't worry about the fact that he wasn't using one-to-one correspondence. It was the counting, and writing with missing numbers which was important. Later, I was called away so Dominic took over the writing. He got up to 450. Then he came in and asked what comes after 999. I told him and he started writing, 1000, 1001, 1002 up to 1006. This sequence must have gone on for at least 30 minutes.

Three weeks later I asked 'Shall I make a line with the cars then you can write them down like we did last time? I've got 10.' He then watched me write the numbers and then continued on his own for a bit, but only went up to 117 this time!

Playing with the parking mat

Had the car parking mat out which we had made a long time ago. He was 4 and a half at the time of this observation. The mat had parking places numbered 1–100. Dominic added numbers up to 141. He had five cars to play with and started a game on which he concentrated for a very long time. He was consistent in his play and totally concentrated on what he was doing. Five cars were placed on spaces 1–5 then he moved first one car to number 10 and then all the cars up so that there were no gaps. He continued until he got to 90 and then lost concentration. Then he wanted me to write down the numbers as he did it; 1–5, 6–10, 11–15, 16–20, 21–25, 26–30, 31–35, 36–40, 41–45, 46–50, 51–55, 56–60, 61–65, 66–70, 71–75, 76–80, 81–85, 86–90. He was totally accurate all the way along.

Next day he had found one other car and so he started the process of going up in 6's. He started to dictate the numbers 1–6, 7–12, 13–18, 19–24. He said, 'It's going a bit different now because we've got a new car. 25–30. I then questioned him as to whether he had got it right. That unfortunately stopped him and he didn't do any more.

Dominic's odes to numbers

Abel's anecdotes end with two complex 'poems' about numbers, made up by Dominic. We don't have room for all of this but here are some samples for you to consider what is going on in the head of this remarkable child.

73 having his tea
74 going to bed
75 morning day
76 getting dressed
77 eating his breakfast
78 playing with his toys
79 going out
80 going to see the balloon.
81 going to school
82 outside
83 going home
84 going to bed
85 having his dinner
86 going out
87 looking after number 65
88 getting dressed in bed
89 playing outside
90 going home
91 going to school
92 getting apples off the tree
93 going to bed
94 looking after number 59
95 going home
96 going to bed
97 getting dressed
98 getting ready
99 getting soon there
100 having his dinner
That's all there is.

 We need to learn to be as alert to children's interest in numbers as we might be in their interest in books or football or anything else.

Here is a lovely set of examples taken from the work of Hughes (2009). They relate to 2-year-old Holly and a set of comments given to the author by the parents of Holly and focused on the child's interest in counting and the language of numbers.

- We had two cups on the table and Holly said she would like 'both of them'. I asked her how many cups there were but she was rather flummoxed by this question. We were also flummoxed that she knew 'both' was for two objects, but didn't seem interested in the fact there were actually two of them.
- Holly refers to (a) couple as 'you two', so Holly's father and I can be addressed as 'you two' as can both her grandparents. I think this is just a phrase to her as she couldn't explain that she's saying it because there are two people.
- When I was peeling an orange recently, Holly asked me if I was 'turning the orange inside out'. When I had finished she wanted to share out the segments so I tried a small experiment of counting a few with her. Together we were able to count there were five although she couldn't give me the answer when I asked afterwards. Holly then ate one of the segments and I asked her to count them again. With great enthusiasm she counted to five again!

(Hughes, pp. 16–17)

 We need to:

- be alert to the language used by children and to the sometimes unvoiced questions behind what they say and do. Children explore systems, including the number system, in their play, their talk, their questions and their drawing;
- develop our own confidence to take the learning about symbols (numbers or letters, words or signs) forward. The best way to do this is the way to do everything with young children: be alert to what children are paying attention to and respectful of their attempts to make sense of whatever it is.

The case study that closes this chapter relates to the seminal work done many years ago with children in Argentina, looking at the hypotheses they were developing, trying out and discarding as they came to terms with the graphic systems used in their communities.

Case Study 7 Coming to understand symbols

This case study is drawn on the important work of Emilia Ferreiro and Ana Teberosky who studied the thinking about graphic and symbolic systems of young children in Argentina. Their work was first published in Spanish in 1979 and they later worked separately or together in

Geneva, Mexico City, Barcelona and Israel. Their book is fascinating and what we reproduce here are some vignettes relating to children's growing understanding of the graphics system. The headings of each section refer to hypotheses developed by the children.

1. Numbers and letters

Two 6-year-old children reflect on their observations of the characteristics of some upper case letters.

Mariano says that 'If I take an M and turn it upside down it is a W; if I turn an A upside down it's an upside down A and I stays the same'.

Alejandro explains that some letters 'have two shapes, it's two in one' and he takes A as an example: 'we take away the little stick and it's this one (V)' (p. 42)

2. Sufficient numbers of characters

The researchers noticed that children appeared to use the number of characters in deciding whether something was readable or not. To test this hypothesis they offered them cards, some with one letter, some with two, some with three and so on up to a maximum of nine characters. The children were also shown cards with one numeral on each. Sometimes the syllables and words on the cards were patterned into traditional combinations used for beginner readers – words like 'papa' for example. The children were asked to sort the cards into 'something-to-read' or 'not-something to read' piles.

Erik (5 years) puts aside the cards with f, e and i (in cursive script) saying that they are not something to read because they have 'only one number'. Then he has some doubts about the cards with two and decides that there must be at least three until finally he settles for at least three.

(p. 29)

Other children-constructed-hypotheses emerged in the research. Having a minimum of three characters is not, in itself, sufficient to make them readable. They must not all be the same. Almost all the children reject something like AAAA as being not readable. Children distinguish between cursive and printed characters in terms of whether they are readable or not.

We end with the explanation of 5-year-old Anabela. She groups the cards with cursive writing and says 'These are not for reading, they are for writing'. In a separate group she places the cards with printed characters or numerals on them and says they are 'for names and also for reading'. Then she removes the cards with numbers on them saying 'They are not for reading because they are letters'. The analysis of the researchers is that her argument is logical since the label she attaches to the characters that are readable is 'numbers'.

All of this gives insight into just what a complex task it is to work out how the symbolic graphic systems operate and how hard children have to work to sort this out.

Summing up

In this chapter we charted the cognitive processes which emerges as children construct and try out their hypotheses about how graphic systems work. We moved on to looking at how learning to write involves more than one process – composing and transcribing – and at the implications of this for what we provide in our settings. We moved on to looking more briefly at children's explorations of another symbolic system – that of numbers.

The implications of all this for practice are obvious and numerous and mostly relate to how we resource our settings to allow for exploration of graphic systems, how we respect children's early attempts and use them as windows into the child's thinking, how we need to know what language(s) are spoken, read and written in the homes of the children so we can relate their attempts to their experience, how we need to offer meaningful contexts for the use of symbolic systems and how we need to model what expert symbols users do.

Chapter 8

War play, cruel play, tragic play

In this chapter we look at children playing roles in order to explore real life and beyond. We look at the rules they draw on, some of which are confusing and contradictory. Here children try out in safety what *might happen if* or replay what has already happened in order to try and make sense of it. In this way they can explore the things that scare and concern them. We also look at what is sometimes called unacceptable play and discuss things like operating a zero tolerance policy with regard to guns and weapons. This is not about play therapy but about play as part of normal life.

> 'I was angry with my friend
> I told my wrath, my wrath did end.
> I was angry with my foe:
> I told it not, my wrath did grow.'
> (William Blake: A Poison Tree)

Actual minds, possible worlds

Many of the definitions of play refer to play as being fun or pleasurable. Anne Haas Dyson (1997) talks of play being about desire and pleasure as children explore possible roles in possible worlds. Whilst there is much to think about in this definition, it seems firmly rooted in a culture which conceives of childhood as a safe and pleasurable phase of life – a privileged culture that is sadly far removed from the real world of millions of the world's children. Even in the Western developed world there are groups of children and individual children who experience real tragedy or trauma or cruelty in their lives. Some of these are caused by other human beings; some are caused by natural events like death from disease; and some by natural disasters. Children who themselves don't suffer such trauma might yet encounter it through images on the television or computer screens or through overhearing disturbing comments. One of the ways in which children try to make sense of such things experienced either directly or more remotely is through playing out their experiences in order to express their feelings and by adopting a range of roles, real and imagined.

Even in the absence of any trauma it is apparent that young children also engage in what might be called unpopular play. They fight, show aggression, display violence and make and use weapons as they play about some of the themes embedded in much literature and much popular and commercial culture. Watch the children in the playground, at home, in the classroom or setting as they set up dramas around chase and escape, attack and defend, stop and capture. The children are engaged in imaginative play and, as Vygotsky noticed, in this play language, ideas and objects can be flexible. We have seen how a stick can be a magic wand or a hobby horse, but it can also be a sword or a lance or a gun. Bruner, in his book *Actual Minds, Possible Worlds*, talks about how children, exposed to the powerful images and themes of popular culture, need to come to understand that 'many worlds are possible, that meaning and reality are created and not dis-covered, that negotiation is the art of constructing new meanings by which individuals can regulate their relations with others' (Bruner, 1986, p. 149).

 We need to find ways of helping children to come to this understanding – that they can make new meanings and be in charge of making change happen.

To do this we may have to re-think our views on types of play that many of us might regard as unacceptable. If we want children to be able to explore not only the real world – the one in which they live their everyday lives – but also all the possible imaginary worlds they hold in their heads, we have to find ways of accepting play that may be unacceptable to us – violent play, gun play, aggressive play, or superhero play, for example. This might mean abandoning the zero tolerance policies often set up in schools and elsewhere. No one is arguing for the unquestioning acceptance of aggression or violence or for children hurting one another.

 We have to find ways of accepting this play whilst still promoting an awareness of an ethical code of how to live harmoniously in communi-ties and groups.

Possible roles in the real world

It is essential to repeat that in the real world children experience many difficult or traumatic events either in their own lives or witnessed through television or other media. In all our schools and settings we will find individual children who have experienced discrimination because of their gender or their colour or their family circumstances or their social class. Being called names or being overlooked is part of the reality of many children's lives. We will also have children who have been abused physically or sexually or emotionally or have witnessed other family members being abused. This is the reality of their lives. We also encounter children whose families are illegal immigrants, or children who have experienced or escaped from war or torture, children who have lived in refugee camps or detention centres. We have children whose parents may have gone off to fight in wars, children who have witnessed fires or bricks thrown through windows. And we will – from time to time – encounter children whose real world has been subject to natural disasters like floods or earthquakes. Most of these children will be impelled to use play (including drawing or writing or music) to try to make sense of these events. There is a mass of evidence of just how children attempt to deal with things like this in their play. You may remember some of the examples of this cited earlier in this book.

Here are some other examples for you to consider. In each case think about whether the child is dealing with the questions 'What if?' or if the child is re-examining something that has happened in the real world. In either case think about whether the child is using the notion of a possible world in the play.

- Edud, who was one of the children to survive the Oklahoma City bombing, repeatedly played 'hospital' using toy figures with missing limbs. The figures were often constructed from Lego and Edud would carefully remove one or more limbs before the play started.

Edud is playing alone, using what is available and adapting that to allow him to play out the trauma he experienced during the bombing where he may have seen people lose their limbs. He spent a considerable amount of time in the real world of hospital.

- Julio's family were driven out of their mobile home during flash floods. At dinner time in his setting he would use broccoli or other vegetables to be trees and pour gravy all over them, flooding the plate.

Julio, too, plays alone and he is clearly re-enacting what he saw during the flood.

- Marianna, who lost her father in the attack on the World Trade Centre, repeatedly played out the horrifying scenes she had seen on TV.

Marianna's teacher said that the little girl came in every morning, went over to the doll's house and repeated the same acts each time – moving the dolls to the windows and throwing them out. She was always silent throughout the play but as soon as she had completed her play moved on to more social activities during which she joined in with others and communicated.

- The children playing in the garden of a setting witnessed an accident in front of their eyes. A motorcyclist was knocked down by a car and was lying on the street, unconscious and bleeding. Soon after, an ambulance came. By this time, everyone in the playground was watching. The paramedics lifted the motorcyclist onto the stretcher, wheeled him into the ambulance and drove away. The children were abnormally quiet. Over the days that followed children started to play 'motorcycle'. One child would drive around on a pretend motorcycle while another would drive a pretend car. They'd crash. The 'motorcyclist' would lie still on the ground. Other children would then try to lift (or drag) the motorcyclist around the playground, while sounding their pretend sirens.

The children, as a group, witnessed the real and disturbing event that took place in front of their eyes, in the real lives of their school playground. Collaboratively they are re-enacting what they have seen and then imagining what might have happened next to the victims.

- Many years ago a community school was set up in Tanzania for the children of activists against the apartheid South African government. The children at SOMAFCO (the school) were either actual orphans or virtual orphans if their parents were fighting or studying elsewhere as part of the struggle. At weekends there was little for the children to do and staff were distressed to find some of the children going out with sharpened sticks, catching animals, killing them and skinning them.

This is a difficult example to analyse because the children's behaviour is not so directly linked to a specific event. Rather it is linked to the lives the children are leading apart from parents and depicts something of their insecurity about the real world in which they are living. This seems a real example of what many would regard as unacceptable play.

 We need to:

- ensure that we know as much as possible about children's experiences before coming to our setting and about their ongoing experiences out of the setting;
- engage with them about their play and build and maintain an ethos of trust and respect

Unacceptable play

It is really difficult to know what to do with the children who endlessly make guns or other weapons, who form gangs and attack one another, who exclude children who are different from them, their play or whose play involves physical or verbal aggression towards others. Many schools and settings, concerned about what seems to be the growing evidence of violence and aggression in our society creeping into the children's lives, introduce zero tolerance policies where gun play, war play and superhero play are all banned. The question of whether this is an appropriate response is important to consider. Children, in their endless search for meaning, try to make sense of the big themes. These include vital issues like right and wrong, good and bad, life and death, power and money, and poverty and war. These are themes that most adults grapple with. Perhaps we need to consider whether children should be allowed to play out their concerns and thoughts and feelings in a safe way. Where a zero tolerance policy is in operation, some children find they are playing in an atmosphere of disapproval. This limits their capacity to fully explore their ideas, their thoughts, their fears and questions. Where then can they take their concerns? You will all be familiar with the child, told not to make or play with guns who, out of sight of the adults, makes anything she finds into a weapon. More than that, children in zero tolerance settings are being expected to operate in a peaceful environment whilst being surrounded by images of violence in the media, in books and stories and sometimes within their homes or communities, sometimes in the most unexpected circumstances. Below is a case study of a young child whose family was anxious for him not to be exposed to any images of aggression. The child then started nursery.

- Michael and Catherine were pacifists and determined that their young son Joshua should not be exposed to images of violence. There was no television in the home and the little boy was firmly denied access to any toy weapons. When he started in the nursery class of his local school, the parents asked the teachers not to let him play with weapons. They tried as best they could but when the other children made guns out of Lego he joined in. One day, on a visit to the library with his mother, Joshua chose a book of Greek legends and insisted that his parents read him at least one before bed every night. The teachers at his nursery contacted the parents to ask what had changed at home, because Joshua suddenly was using every opportunity and every piece of equipment in the nursery to make swords. In his determined, logical and serious attempts to understand the battles between good and evil, right and wrong, strong and weak, he took on different roles and involved others in his play.

Penny Holland (2003) has addressed the issue of the effectiveness of zero tolerance policies and suggests that where such policies are abandoned, children's play can be enhanced, their understanding of complex issues developed and their abilities to find solutions to problems increased. Her work is interesting and easy to read. One of the things she found in her research was that aspects of play, particularly of construction play (often the setting for the making of weapons) in settings no longer operating zero tolerance policies, became more prolonged, more cooperative, more serious and involved children using more spoken language than in settings operating a negative attitude to gun play. Holland argues that once the disapproval is removed, children relax into building whatever they chose to build (guns and all) with greater freedom. Holland insists that she never advocates that children should be offered manufactured toy weapons in schools and settings because these dictate the nature of the play. However, where children choose to use available materials to make a weapon, it is because they have the need to explore something: it has not been imposed on them. In this play they are moving from the concrete (the real weapon in the form of a toy) to the abstract (something that stands for the weapon). Vygotsky, as you know, believed that whilst children are initially bound by the concrete world (the real world of things and people they can see and touch and hear), in play, particularly imaginative play, they can move beyond the concrete. What happens is that the child begins to act independently from what she sees.

> In play thought is separated from objects and action arises from ideas rather than from things: a piece of wood begins to be a doll and a stick becomes a horse.
>
> (Vygotsky, 1978, p. 96–7)

Holland also observes that where adults engage with children about their constructions, children's comments often show a concern with real issues such as the differences between good or bad, between fair and unfair, between equal and unequal, between weak and strong. Here are some of the things children have been heard to say about the weapons they have made, gathered from a range of observation notes.

- 'If you press this button it goes peow and kills people and if you press this button it goes brrr and makes everybody alive.' (Holland, 2003, p. 83)
- 'It's not really a sword. Well it is. It will kill the man because he is greedy and has all the gold, but it will turn the man who is poor into a prince. So it is a sort of magic sword.'
- 'I made a light saver that shoots out flames to burn up the giant so the boy can take the magic toys.'
- 'This is a sort of flying machine. These bits here shoot out bullets to kill the bad guys. I haven't made the other bit of the machine yet. That's the one that shoots out money for the goodies.'
- 'It is a gun but it is a good gun. It only kills monsters.'

It is evident that where adults engage with children about any aspects of their play, they are able constantly to reinforce a culture and ethos of non-violence and cooperation without having to ban anything. The practitioners who offered the above examples also explained how they responded to them. Here are the words said by the children followed by the response of the adult.

> 'It's not really a sword. Well it is. It will kill the man because he is greedy and has all the gold, but it will turn the man who is poor into a prince. So it is a sort of magic sword.'

> I said something like 'That's really interesting. I wonder if it is fair to kill someone who is greedy and has all the gold. Perhaps you think about how you could persuade him to share his gold with the poor people. What do you think?' I wanted to raise some questions in the child's mind about violence as the only solution.

> 'I made a light saver that shoots out flames to burn up the giant so the boy can take the magic toys.'

> I wanted to suggest an alternative reading of a story, possibly offering the child my own 'What if?' question. So I said something like 'I wonder if that is the giant in the Jack and the Beanstalk story. In my version of the story he does get killed when he tries to climb down the beanstalk after Jack. I am always quite sad about that because I think he might really be quite a nice giant.' (My hidden question 'What if he was a nice giant?') Perhaps he is lonely and needs a friend.

> 'This is a sort of flying machine. These bits here shoot out bullets to kill the bad guys. I haven't made the other bit of the machine yet. That's the one that shoots out money for the goodies'.

> My response to this was quite brusque because this child is always talking about bullets and killing and I find that annoying. Perhaps I could have handled it better but what I said was 'I really don't like machines that shoot bullets because bullets kill people. I think that maybe bad guys can sometimes be good guys.

> 'It is a gun but it is a good gun. It only kills monsters.'

> I decided to challenge his assumption that all monsters are bad. So I said 'Ah, monsters. A gun that kills monsters. I once made up a friendly monster – one who looked really scary but underneath was really kind. I wonder if you have ever met a monster like that? I wanted the child to think about things like how things and people who don't look good may be good underneath.

We should think of ways in which to respond to children's making of weapons and challenge, positively, their comments.

One way is to raise questions of your own (as we have seen in the examples above). Another is to base the questions on 'What if?' possibilities. We are trying to take children from real worlds to possible worlds.

Exploring tragedy in real life

Where children are allowed to play at anything, we see changes in the complexity of the play and of the language used. In classrooms and settings that operate a policy of allowing children to talk about anything that concerns them something similar emerges. The children respond to this openness with a willingness to share their own experiences, fears, thoughts, dreams and desires. The sharing takes place in different ways: through talk, drawings, drama and role play, the representation and re-representation of actual and possible worlds.

Many years ago, in an infant class in an inner London school, before the imposition of the national curriculum or the strategies, the staff and children built a classroom ethos of trust and respect. The children talked to one another and to the adults about dozens of aspects of their lives – what they had watched on television, who had come to play after school, what mum had said when the baby dropped a cup and broke it, how mum and dad argued at the table, what happened when an older sibling stole some money, what they had seen on their way to school. Sometimes a significant event, seen on television, demanded more in-depth discussion.

In 1988, the disaster of the sinking of the ferry at Zeebrugge had been witnessed by many of the children on television and their discussion and subsequent drawing and writing and role play were revealing. All the children had something to say – some had been on ferries, some knew someone who had missed that particular ferry and many were worried that it might happen again and in particular might happen to them and those they loved. In the open atmosphere of that particular class children could choose many ways to deal with and reflect on their concerns. Fiona and Alex had both been on ferries to France and both chose to draw pictures of people in the bar as the water started to pour in. Alex accompanied his drawing with a running commentary:

> When we went to France we had croissants for breakfast. That's what you have when you go to France ... These are the trays of salad and they are going to fall off – SPLAT! into the water. All the plates and cups and knives and things are just smashing off the tables and here's the water starting to come in ... This man, here, this one, he's just falling against

the wall and it hurts – OW! And here's the man, the one, you know, he made himself a bridge so that people could get out. My dad said if it happened to us, first we would save the baby, then me, then my mum and then my dad.

At this point he was interrupted by Fiona who said 'No! If that ever happens to us my mum PROMISES that she will be saved first. I wouldn't want to be alive without my mum'.

(Smidt, observation notes 1988)

Even a casual reading of that is moving and indicative of just how deeply children think about the things that frighten them. The children in this example were aged 6 and 7. Both included speech bubbles in their drawings and what the people were shown to be saying shows how appropriately these young children were able to take on the views and the feelings of others. Fiona has a man and his son in the water and the man says 'Swim to me, son' to which the boy replies 'OK'. Alex has the man making a bridge of his body for others to walk over whilst a child standing beside him says 'You can do it, dad!'

Later, that same day groups of children were seen involved in very dramatic role play re-enacting the drama they had witnessed on TV, discussed in the class and drawn pictures about. In the home corner a group of children were playing out the sinking of the ferry, using the home corner equipment to replicate the bar that Alex had talked about and with children playing the roles of adults and children on the ferry. One child is chosen to be the one who makes his body into a bridge and there is much negotiation about who is 'light' enough to walk across him and be saved. There is a very dramatic scene of children pretending to be engulfed by the rising water and crying for help.

The play extended over several days and became more and more elaborate as different scenarios were discussed and re-enacted. One scenario included children making a special boat out of milk crates tied to some tyres and the children spent many hours trying to make this clumsy structure mobile. The same children later used the water tray with containers and small world toys to attempt to show a rescue. Some children played at a funeral in the playground. Most moving was a long discussion between two children, seemingly playing randomly in the water tray, but discussing how it was possible for water to be heavy enough to capsize something as big as a boat or a ferry. Pouring water from container to container as they talked, they finally came to the conclusion that the ferry must have capsized because all the lorries and cars and slipped to one side making the ferry unstable.

 We must listen to children and respond to what they bring. All themes must be allowed.

Not too young to learn

Young children are often observed saying and doing unacceptable things. When this is mentioned to their parents, the excuse is that they are 'too young to understand'. But the behaviour of one child can impact negatively on another and it is clear that this is not acceptable. So we have to refer back to the research which shows that young children do understand that other people have feelings and thoughts and find ways of not accepting such behaviour. In this book, you have already encountered examples of children refusing to play with other children for one reason or another; girls not being able to play at what they want to play at; children being excluded because they are seen as being different in some way. In many settings adults work hard to redress this and spend time ensuring that the language they use is not offensive or discriminatory, that they pay attention to and respect the experiences and cultures and languages and abilities of their pupils.

Some of the most interesting work with regard to this involves the use of Persona Dolls. Developed by Babette Brown, these dolls are life-like and small child-size cloth figures each with his or her own individual identity, life history, family and cultural background, likes and dislikes, fears and abilities. You can buy boy and girl dolls, dolls dressed in clothes to reflect their religions and customs, dolls that are obese or wear glasses or are missing a limb. The dolls can be used as a practical tool to promote psychosocial development and emotional literacy for children and to address discrimination, anti-bias, diversity and inclusion. The dolls and training in their use are currently offered in the UK and in South Africa.

Here is one case study to illustrate how the doll can be used:

A teacher in a North London primary school was told that a child in the reception class was starting to refuse to come to school in the mornings. After much discussion between the teacher and the parents and the child it emerged that the little boy, Alex, was being drawn into rough play by the other boys in his class. Alex was a gentle and quiet child who hated fighting and shouting, but when he, on one occasion, refused to join in, the other children called him names and made him very unhappy. The teacher had been on Persona Doll training and she decided to use this in an attempt to make the group understand that all people have rights and should be treated with respect to their feelings. She borrowed a white boy doll, wearing glasses like Alex and carefully prepared what she would say. At story time she gathered the children around her and introduced them to her doll, whose name was David. The children had not encountered a Persona Doll before and were intrigued by its size, lifelike appearance and the doll's history which the teacher told them. She said that he was an only child, that he loved to hear stories and play on his Wii and that he liked playing board games and dressing up. She then told the story of how, one day, he went to the park where three other boys started to tease him about wearing glasses, about not being 'strong' and not playing what they called 'proper boy games'. He tried to get away but they punched him and he fell on the ground, where he was kicked and punched again. At this point in the story the group became very quiet. The teacher stopped telling the story and asked the children if they would like to take over and find a happy ending. Some of the girls had suggestions about going to fetch his mum or giving him a hug, but one of the little boys responsible for taunting Alex came up with this: 'I think maybe David could ask one of the boys to come to his house to play on his Wii. Then they could make friends', whilst another culprit added 'Maybe he should just tell those bullies that he likes doing other things and doesn't want to play rough games. Maybe they could find a game of something like dragons instead of fighting that they could all play together'.

There are, of course, no magic answers, no quick fixes. Children bully and are bullied and this is a serious issue for all of us. No incidents of bullying should be ignored or dismissed and children's rights to be themselves should be insisted on. The use of drama, storying, and props like the Persona Dolls are all techniques worth trying.

Inventing rules in play

We have seen how children, in their role play and exploration of symbolic systems, work out, use and make up rules. As they get older and more adept at inventing rules they play complex games, sometimes alone but often in collaboration, to act out and explore their dangerous feelings and their fears and anxieties.

- After a death in the family 6-year-old Rosa Mae invented a complicated game called 'Hurt me'. She invented the game when she found some sticky labels which her mum said she could use. This game involved her in making a series of labels (see Figure 8.1) on which she wrote instructions. All of these involved instructions, telling someone to do something to her, often to hurt her and sometimes to comfort her. So they said things like 'Kick me and hit me' or 'Hug me and kiss me'. She spent an afternoon at the kitchen table making the labels and took them into her class the next day. A number of her friends were interested in joining her game and she explained the rules like this: 'We put them all upside down on the table and take turns to pick them up. When we have picked them all up the one with the most kind ones is the loser and the ones with the most nasty ones is the winner'. The teaching assistant

Figure 8.1 One of Rosa Mae's 'nasty' instructions.

in Rosa Mae's class, witnessing the game, was very aware of the fact that Rosa Mae's definition of the rules insisted that the winner would be the person collecting the most nasty instructions. She noted that Rosa Mae played the game throughout the whole of one week and only then was she able to move on to more positive things.

- Street children in Delhi were observed playing their own game of shops. The counter was made of an old tin supported on an old wooden crate and the children were selling odds and ends to one another. For currency they were using empty cigarette packets and the rules they devised involved assigning amounts to money to the different brands of cigarettes.
- Games of marriage are commonly seen in settings both urban and rural and the rules that apply are those that apply to the place and the group within which the play is based.
- Some brides have to wear red; others wear white; others are completely hidden from view.

Understanding rules is important in belonging to a family or a group, a society and a community. There is some evidence that even very young children can make moral judgements. Judith Smetana carries out some research with children as young as 2 and a half, presenting them with everyday scenarios. In some of these a child broke a rule in the preschool – perhaps refusing to hang their coats up, eat their lunch, and tidy up at tidying up time. In other scenarios the broken rules caused some real physical or psychological damage to another child. So here one child might be hitting or teasing another child or taking something that belonged to someone else. The children were asked how bad these transgressions were and whether the children concerned should be punished. Most significantly Smetana asked the questions: would this action be all right if it happened in a setting with different rules? Would this action be all right if the rules were different? In effect these questions were asking the children to decide if it would be OK to not eat your lunch or to hit a child if the teacher said it was OK. Even these very young children understood the differences between breaking rules where there were no personal consequences and breaking rules where someone got hurt. One of the most startling things about this research is that even children who had been abused knew that hurting people was fundamentally wrong.

The following case study is relevant and moving. Read it and see.

Case Study 8 In memory of Jackie Kirk

It is difficult to clearly link this case study with the title of this chapter, but it is included here because it highlights some of the difficulties faced by our fellow practitioners in less privileged societies. Jackie Kirk, an aid worker in refugee camps, was tragically killed with other members of the International Rescue Committee in 2008 in Afghanistan. A tribute to her and her work appeared in *Early Childhood Matters* (November 2008) which talks of an initiative known as The Healing Classrooms which was implemented in Kunana, Ethiopia. Examining existing provision in the refugee camp, it was recognised that a new building was needed and the programme put in place drew heavily on the experience of Save the Children, Sweden, which had developed a preschool programme for refugee children in the Western Sudanese camps in Ethiopia. The programme aids to teach entirely through play, role play, music, art and storytelling. Literacy and numeracy are integrated into any project. One of the difficulties of successfully implementing the programme is the lack of appropriate training for staff. It is stated that teachers still tend to stick to standing at the front of the room in order to try to hold the attention of the young children as they might do with older children.

But some good things are happening and the children are beginning to learn a host of important things through their experience. The article talks about how the children benefit from having more space, and more than that, from having space which is their own. It also talks of how the young children are coming together with others from different ethnic groups and learning to live and play together. They are building a sense of self-identity and of group identity but also coming to understand about difference and similarities. There is a strong emphasis on health and well-being and the name 'Healing Classrooms' comes about because it aims to work within the principles of social well-being and healing and to tie these together through good and appropriate teaching. There is still a long way to go, but much is being achieved.

Summing up

In this chapter we looked at play which cannot be described as pleasurable or fun. We have looked at how children use to play to express their thoughts and feelings about painful personal experiences, about frightening second-hand experiences, and about negative imagined experiences. In doing this we have looked at how children play out the questions 'What if ...?' We have touched on aspects of unacceptable play and at the beginnings of the ability to make moral judgements.

The implications for practice include helping children come to know that through their play and storying they can make new meanings. We need to know as much as possible about children's lives before and out of the setting and we need to engage with them (always sensitively) about their play and do this in a setting in which trust and respect are embedded. We need to consider whether or not to allow guns and aggressive play and discuss our decisions with parents and carers.

Chapter 9

Why play matters
Voices

This final chapter summarises what has been said about how to explicitly recognise the importance of play as a serious and essential mode of learning for both very young children and older children. It looks at what practitioners do to promote play in classrooms and settings and at how other people involved in the lives and learning of children can be persuaded that what children do is not 'just play'. The voices are those of practitioners and others as they explain their thinking. They are the voices we should listen to.

> 'The teacher just opens the door: the learner must walk through'.
>
> (Chinese proverb)

> 'Education either functions as an instrument which is used to facilitate integration of the younger generation into the logic of the present system and bring about conformity or it becomes the practice of freedom, the means by which men and women deal critically and creatively with reality and discover how to participate in the transformation of their world.'
>
> (Paulo Freire)

A playful pedagogy?

This is a book about play and it has been written at this time in order to confirm practitioners in their belief that play is one of the prime ways in which children learn about their world and those who live in it. Play is often conceived of as something rather lovely and slight and trivial, and this is perhaps because the emphasis in much of the writing to date has focused on play as pleasurable being what children do when they are given choice. The truth is more complex than that, and practitioners do need to understand very clearly just what it is about play that makes it something so potentially powerful as a mode of learning and something that applies to all children, privileged or not.

The quotation from Paulo Freire that opens this chapter says something very important to all those interested in children and learning. He was a brilliant and respected educationalist from Brazil who was concerned primarily with the education of the millions of illiterate adults he encountered in his teaching. Like us all, Freire was operating in a context and he was aware and critical of the extremes of wealth and poverty, opportunity and lack of opportunity embedded in his society and in many others. You can see from the words he has written about the purposes of education that he feels strongly that all those being educated should be educated not to fit in and be unquestioning, but rather to be critical, thoughtful and active in reforming things to make them better. The 'method' he advocated was known as the dialogical method and it was aimed at enabling peasants in Brazil to be able to 'read the world' as well as to read the word. In essence he was seeking to educate people to become conscious of their presence and potential power in changing things about their world that they did not like. The implications of this are that learners should not be passive but active in not only understanding their world but acting on it.

If you accept this it follows that practitioners who encourage children to ask questions, seek to find answers and learn how to share their thoughts with others are building critical, thoughtful and potentially transformative adults. One of the questions practitioners must know the answer to is what sort of education they want to offer – one which encourages repetition and conformity or one that promotes questioning and creativity. Those who want the latter will be considering how to offer a pedagogy – a way of teaching – that will encourage learners to remain playful. Goouch (2009) calls this 'a playful pedagogy'.

By this stage in your reading you will have thought about play which is serious, difficult and sometimes exploring deeply traumatic experiences and recognised that definitions of play which talk about it being pleasurable are, at best, incomplete. Lip service is paid to the importance of play in the early years, but an analysis of what goes on in many classrooms and settings leads to the conclusion that teachers and practitioners may re-interpret and re-shape play in order to use it to justify existing practice. At present there are discussions about how it is possible to talk of adult-directed play because it is the adults who control the learning environment. This is true and no one is ignoring the vital role that practitioners have in play. But playful practitioners will be those who provide the contexts and arrange the environment primarily to allow the children to be in charge of what they do, where they do it, how they do it and with whom. Goouch argues powerfully that it is both possible and desirable, certainly in the early years, but hopefully beyond, to develop and maintain 'a pedagogy steeped in play and led by children and to create classroom cultures that allow children to spend time learning before they encounter classrooms bounded by a culture of performance, driven by testing and results' (p. 141). This is an important assertion.

Goouch insists that young children need to be in classrooms where their curriculum is steeped in play. More than that, those who work with these children need to understand the significance of play and to be able to explain it to their colleagues and to parents and carers. Being an early years practitioner requires immense sensitivity, the ability to attend carefully to what children do and say, genuine respect for children and the work they do as they make sense of and act on the world and willingness to learn. Moreover, since we know that in the early years there is enormous brain growth and the development of synaptic connections, meaning that children are learning a great deal in a short space of time, practitioners also need to be:

- *responsive* (so that they both take notice of what children are interested in and paying attention to and where appropriate, engage in conversation with them about this);
- *intersubjective* (so that they intuit or work out what children are paying attention to or feeling, and respectful so that children can develop a genuine two-way relationship with them); and
- *interactive* (so that they can engage with children as they play and follow the lead given by the playing child).

Goouch goes on to suggest that practitioners should find ways to create contexts (based on the observed interests of children) which allow them to *follow the child into play* and then, alongside the child, co-construct the play. This may involve considerations of the following:

(a) resourcing;
(b) narrative, or
(c) storying.

Let us take a look at each of these in turn.

(a) Context and resourcing
Stig Brostrom (1997) talks of what he calls 'Frame Play', which is basically role play, where the children negotiate with one another about the roles they will play, the theme of the play and formulate what Elkonin (1980) calls 'a plot'. The plot is what the children draw on in the play scenario in terms of their own experiences and how these are orchestrated. Certain skills are involved in this and they include the following:
- the ability *to distinguish between the real world and their world of pretence*;
- the ability to *choose a play theme collaboratively* and accept that this might change as the play progresses;
- the *ability to make, agree, share and abide by the rules* relating to their play.

For Brostrom, frame play goes beyond role play because it involves the presence in some senses of a teacher or practitioner. So he believes that frame play takes place where *a practitioner is a partner in the play*. The easiest way of understanding this is thinking about play that arises after some shared experience initiated by an adult (this is best arising out of the observed interests of the children). So obvious things like an outing to the post office or clinic or market; a walk in the park or the wood; an outing to a place of interest to the children; a story the children have been told or read; the celebration of rituals and festivals; or the visit of someone to the setting. Here are some examples:

- In India at Melas children enact important figures in Hindu religious stories through songs and dance and mime and puppetry. Here stories are told about kings and queens and noble people. After the ceremony in which all the children have been involved, a puppetry workshop takes place where a puppet maker from the town comes into the setting and helps the children use found, natural and cheap materials to make their own puppets. The adults in the setting also make puppets and then use these in the stories they invent and share.
- There is a new child in the nursery whose father is a fireman. The children seem really interested in this and so the staff decided to build something out of this. The children have been taken to the local fire station, where Bilaal's father now works, and when they returned to the setting the practitioners who had accompanied them on the visit ensured that they made available some tools which might enhance the play. They provided a telephone, a walkie-talkie, a desk, a hose, a ladder, some buckets and some protective helmets.

Becoming a play partner is something that some practitioners do with ease but others find difficult to do. There is no requirement to become a play partner in the sense of having to adopt a role in the play: play partners in this sense are partners only in terms of setting up and resourcing activities.

Resources can be important to children's play, but this does not mean that they have to be expensive or specially made. There are many examples of children making dolls and cars out of clay, human figures out of rags, vehicles and figures out of wire, pretend food out of seeds and mud, plates out of leaves, furniture out of tin and so on. You know that Vygotsky believed that signs and symbols and tools all have a mediating function. Children can use them for their real purposes (a chair to sit on) or for purposes that they devise (a chair as part of a fire engine). Any tool has been made by people as a way of helping them and others regulate their interactions with the real world. A pen, for example, is a tool designed by human beings to help them record their thoughts to share with others. A stick in wet sand can do the same. A knife, designed by human beings, is a tool to help people make large things smaller. A sharp stone can do the same. A hose, designed by human beings, is a tool to help people allow liquids to be transported from one spot to another. Let us return to the previous examples to see how, in play, children's actions are mediated by the tools they use.

- In the example of the play that took place after the festival, the making of the puppets (where the children used the resources to create new things) was what allowed the children to use what they had made to create entirely new play scripts and scenarios.
- In the play that took place after the visit and which was stimulated by the tools offered back at the setting, there were clear examples of how the objects were used to determine and affect the play. One child at play chose to use the phone to call the 'chief'; another used the ladder to rescue someone; two little girls used the walkie-talkie to stay in touch with one another and discuss the fire they were dealing with and a group used the hose to put the fire out.

In both examples children were able to make links between their external actions (using the artefacts) and their thinking (the actions or roles they chose and agreed to play).

A reminder that we should become skilled at noticing what the children are interested in so that we can use these interests to create contexts. We then need to follow the lead of the children and where appropriate join in the play. All intervention must be sensitive and remain focused on the child's agenda and not chase pre-determined goals.

The first voice we encounter in this chapter is that of Rehana, who is a teacher in a nursery school in Hackney.

'When I tell children to do something they will do it but hardly ever concentrate on it for very long. When I introduce a context in the room based on what even one child has shown an interest in and leave it to the children to choose what to do in there I notice that they can play at something for hours on end and concentrate really hard. Often I talk to them about what they are doing and we end up having really good discussions. I am convinced that when they can follow their own interests they are learning much more than when they follow my instructions. I am persuaded that play makes sense.'

(b) Narrative and storying

Goouch looked at practitioners who used storying in their practice and analysed this in terms of what she called 'playful pedagogy'. You know that storying is what happens when children invent or make up stories for their own purposes. This is explicitly not when children make up a story because they have been told to. The story may or may not be recorded in some way.

That decision is up to the child. We have encountered storying earlier in this book in the work of Dyson and Paley. Here we will look at what Gooch discovered in her small-scale research into this. There were two practitioners involved, both committed to play, respectful of children, and aware of the significance of power relationships between adults and children. They could choose to join in the play, talk to the children, listen to the children, respond to the children and respect what they were saying.

Goouch found that there were some significant differences between the two practitioners.

- J initiated, modelled, participated and became a willing play partner. She seemed to be overlaying her views on those of the children, drawing the children into her assumptions of shared understanding. She often talked over the activity, narrating what was happening.
- M observed more than participated in play and left respectful silences. She asked questions without expecting answers and regarded the child as expert.

  Both practitioners described themselves as being reluctant to shape children's views. Goouch concluded that both acted as guides rather than leaders.

The next voice is that of Meena, who is a nursery nurse in a children's centre.

'My role in play? Well mostly to listen and look and work out what the child is interested in and doing. Then sometimes I say something to try and let the child know that I have worked out what her focus of attention is. Sometimes I get this wrong, but I am getting better at it. I try not to ask questions but to make comments and any questions I do ask are questions whose answers I don't have in my head. They are questions which come out of what I have noticed and the answers to the questions are important to me. They are not to test the child!'

The role of the adult in play discourses

In play, particularly in fantasy play, pretend play, role play or sociodramatic play (various terms to describe more or less the same thing), children revisit their previous experiences and interactions and re-interpret, sometimes making changes or refinements or moving on from them. The child, who is the teller of the tale, or the writer of the script or the owner of the discourse, is in control and either alone or more usually in negotiation with her play partners she/they decide what will happen, in what order and how it will end. Neither the play script nor structure are fixed and may easily change in response to what emerges as the play starts. In the emerging play children make evident what is in their minds as they explore significant people and events.

The play scripts and discourses can be extremely complex, with different narratives weaving in and out. The children involved in any play event can be described as forming what Mercer (2000) calls a 'community of discourse'. For him and for others, *dialogue* and *talk* are very significant features of play and learning and often require the sensitive and respectful involvement of adults. It is very important to remember that adults should ensure that if they do intervene they do it following the child's lead and that they do not hijack the child's agenda and impose their own goals on the process.

We hear now the voice of Willyanna, a teaching assistant in a school in Bradford.

'I used to go over to where someone was doing something – drawing a picture, say, and ask in a very friendly voice "Oh what have you drawn? It is lovely!" Then I went on a course about play and learned that all I was doing was showing the child I had no idea at all of what she was interested in. So now I do it differently – or at least I think I do. For example, yesterday I noticed that one of the children had made some very strange looking shapes out of clay. I went over and sat there for a while and watched and I noticed that the child seemed to be trying to fit legs onto a large body shape and the legs were too thin to hold the weight of the body. After a while I said "Would you like to try putting some of these thin wooden sticks inside each of the legs so that they are stronger?" She beamed at me and nodded, so I knew that I had worked it out correctly. This time my intervention helped.'

Some practitioners insist that they only intervene in fantasy or imaginative play if they notice that one or more children are being discriminated against by the others. Other practitioners think that the best way of handling incidents like these is by engaging the children involved in discussion after the play.

Mindy Blaise, in her examination of gender discourses in an early childhood classroom, noted many examples of gender discrimination and the acting out of stereotypical gender roles. Most fascinating is her study of Alan, a 5-year-old Anglo-American boy from a stable home and having an older brother. The class teacher tells Blaise that Alan is so like his father that seeing them together makes you understand all of Alan's classroom behaviour. Blaise notices that he disregards anything feminine, from girls themselves to the colour pink. He has internalised definite attitudes about the roles of boys and girls and insists on these in his classroom discourse and in his play. Blaise finds her own response to the child disturbing. She says she feels and acts as though he is the only child in her study and manages, in every situation, to grab her attention. For her, the implications for practitioners are clear. Such assured masculinity that demands the attention of the adults and takes their attention away from others, particularly from the girls, is not acceptable.

We hear now the voice of Glenda who is a member of staff in a play-group in Suffolk.

'The children were playing inside a tent set up in the garden. The play had been ongoing for about 45 minutes when I heard shouts and went over to see what was happening. I found Toby pushing Marion to one side, shouting "I am the man, here. I am the man and I am the one who decides. That is what I do!" Marion, tears streaming down her cheeks was insisting, "But it was my idea. We were playing here before you came in and you are spoiling it for us." I decided I had to intervene so asked Toby to come with me: he did so but very reluctantly. As we left, the girls resumed their play. I took Toby into the room and we sat at table and I asked him if he thought it was fair to interrupt the play and take over. He insisted that he just wanted to play and that the girls "need me to be the father, cos I am strong". I wondered what models of fathering he had, and said "My dad is very strong, but also very kind. When we need someone strong sometimes he helps us, but my mum is also strong and she helps us too." He looked at me in disbelief. "Your mum? But she's a girl". It feels as though I am bashing my head against a brick wall – I have to do this so often. But maybe, in the long term, boys like Toby will begin to look at the world differently. None of this is his fault, of course. He is just playing out what he sees in his world and trying to make sense of what's for boys and what for girls. Someone needs to challenge this.'

Making space and time for play

Nurseries and settings are usually organised so that there is space for children to play both indoors and out. This is not always the case in reception classes and certainly not in other classrooms. A pedagogy based on play really needs practitioners and teachers to consider carefully how the space is organised. Children need space in which to explore their interests and many rooms contain too much furniture and not enough space between the pieces of furniture. Remember that young children (and many older children) need to move regularly rather than being confined to sitting down passively for long periods of time. At the very least a play setting should include enough space for children to construct things (out of blocks or Lego or found materials), to make things (out of found and made materials), to explore the effects of movement, to engage in exploratory play with sand and water and other materials, to play collaboratively in areas of the room, to set up contexts for role play based on children's interests and experience and to paint. These all require large open areas, but children also need small private areas where they can giggle in pairs, hide, look at a book alone or with another.

Operating a play-based curriculum carries enormous implications for the organisation of the day and might require some serious discussion with headteachers and managers. Children, given the freedom to choose, often choose to do things in which they get deeply engrossed. This means that they pay great attention to what they are doing. Interrupting this by demanding that all the children stop what they are doing and go to assembly or PE or out to play is disrespectful to their needs and does little to help them continue to be people who can become deeply involved in solving a problem they have identified or expressing their thoughts and feelings. So children need long, unbroken periods of time and also need to be able to return to what they were doing on one day on the next day and then on the day after that. Sometimes expressing what you feel or solving a problem you have set demands a great deal of time.

Roberto, a newly qualified teacher in a reception class in Argyle says:

'For me time and space are crucial. When I talked to the headteacher about getting rid of some of the furniture in the classroom to make more space for large-scale work and exploration she was horrified. But I invited her to come and have a look after I moved some of the equipment out and she was persuaded. Getting her to agree to us not coming to assemblies or leaving the room to do PE was more difficult. I had to promise that I would ensure that children were having plenty of physical exercise during the day and that I attended to their spiritual health through all the contexts on offer. And we do that in our class. Our contexts have included a herb garden outdoors where we have planted herbs and we look after them and go out to see how they are growing and use them in our cooking. We talk about where plants come from and how they grow. We have had a clinic and a gym and other things all at the suggestion of the children.'

Is it 'just play'?

One of the major problems facing practitioners who understand just how powerful play can be as a way of learning is to make their colleagues, the media, those in government and the parents understand just why play in learning matters. For many years educationalists talked of play as being 'children's work' and it was common to hear groups of parents cite this as justification for their nursery-aged children 'just playing'. Play and work are both alike in some ways and different in others. If we conceive of play as being serious and sometimes difficult, it is easier to see it as children's work. But what makes play so unique is the freedom it gives the child to follow up her own concerns.

Lancy (1977) in his work in Sierra Leone found that play has definite relationships to work. We hear his voice now and what he says makes us take a step back and think again about this.

> 'I didn't find that play has no relationship to work. They are, to use a favourite anthropological term, "integrated" ... make-believe play seems to be one step in an alternatively collapsing and expanding process. A child of three spends hours observing a blacksmith at work. A child of four brings his stick down on a rock repeatedly and says he is a blacksmith. A child of eight weaves with his friends an elaborate reconstruction of the blacksmith's craft, all in make-believe. A child of ten is a blacksmith's helper in reality: he fetches wood for the forge and no more. At twelve he begins learning the actual skills of smithing, adding a new one every few months or so... . (p. 87).

This is a fascinating account of how these children, through playing out aspects of the real world, go into possible worlds only to return to the real world later. There are links between work and play and children play at being workers as they play at being many other things. If we emphasise only the self-chosen nature of play without talking also about how serious it is in terms of learning, we will not persuade everyone of the value of play. There are many parents throughout the world who cannot afford the luxury of contemplating having choice, and for them the idea of children playing at school is anathema.

Clara, who is head of a children's centre in Manchester said:

> 'I got fed up with the parents of the four-year-olds in our middle class centre coming up and complaining that their children were not reading and writing yet. They were, as they said, 'just playing'. I had given them endless leaflets and handouts about the importance of play and then decided to organise a play day. I invited all the parents of the older children to come along, told them to wear old clothes and be prepared to get their hands dirty. I called in the help of friends from across the borough so there were lots of adults around to explain and talk to parents. The workshops started at nine in the morning and went on till nine at night in the hope that we would attract some working parents. We used three large rooms and there was an educator in each. In one room we had set up a domestic play scenario with lots of reading and writing equipment and a scenario to stimulate play. The scenario created was a troubling one – the disappearance of a small child. In the next room we had construction equipment and there was a sign-up saying "Take care. Wear hard hats. Danger of collapse" and in the third room we had paints and easels, clay and clay tools, junk materials for modelling and so on. All the parents were told that they had to do

something with at least one other person and that they could move from room to room whenever they were ready. No restrictions on numbers. No timetable. Lots of space and potential problems to solve. It was fantastic! A week later they were invited to a meeting to share their feelings (and have tea and cake!). They had all gone home exhausted and all were helped to see how they had solved problems, negotiated with others, shared, read instructions, written things, made things and so on.'

Adults and the provision of models

One of the things practitioners can think about is the provision of models of learning and behaviour for the children. The practitioner herself or himself is often a model. This is done through many of the normal activities of the day – reading to the children, writing for them, being helpful and friendly and comforting and polite, using pencils or pairs of scissors of other material tools and so on. Every time children encounter an adult doing something, they are seeing what an expert reader, writer, user of materials, human being does. It is important to remember, too, how children learn from one another, and often this learning takes place through play.

Now we hear, for the first time, the voice of a student teacher, Vidya.

'We had been on a visit to the local art gallery to look at an exhibition of carpets from Turkey. There are many children in my unit who are Turkish. Whilst we were there there was a weaver actually in the gallery and the children were fascinated by her weaving. I then remembered that I had a tiny handloom at home from a weaving class I had been on so the next day I went into the nursery with my loom and sat there weaving. All the children came up to watch and to talk to me about what I was doing and the next day I left the loom out and the children were allowed to use it (under supervision, at the insistence of the teacher). What we ended up with was a collaborative weaving – something many children had had a part in making and we hung it on the wall and next to it I put up some of the wonderful things the children said when they were weaving or watching the weaving. We all loved it.'

Charting and documenting play

Children are learning all the time, at home, at school or setting, in the community. They learn from every experience (good or bad) and every interaction (good or bad). The younger children learn an enormous amount through the routines of the day when they are inevitably engaged in interaction with others.

We now hear the voice of Paola who is a teacher or pedagogista in an Italian crèche. She is thinking about why it is important to document what children do in their play and this is what she says:

'The parents who leave their very young children with us often feel sad that they miss out on key moments in their child's development. We have a policy of charting all aspects of development each day and putting these up on display for all parents to see. Our focus is on something significant that has happened. I love doing this. It feels so positive to write something (and take a photo sometimes) and put it up for all to see. Yesterday I noticed that 2-year-old Lorenzo held hands with his friend Mario and they held hands all morning as they played outside and when it was dinner time they had a discussion about how they could eat with one hand so they didn't have to let go of one another's hands. To me it seemed a beautiful moment of social and emotional development, with a problem (eating one-handed) embedded in it. Taking notes of significant moments is a really important part of operating a pedagogy based on play and relationships. It seems to me the only way you can collect evidence of just how children learn through play and through relationships. I recommend it to everyone.'

And they lived happily ever after ...

It seems fitting to end the book with the voice of someone who has spent her entire adult professional life working to ensure that children can play out their concerns. In her book called *Bad Guys Don't Have Birthdays*, Vivian Gussin Paley charts the changes to her thinking as an educator which allowed her to arrive at the place where she was able to write a book based entirely on her observations of 4-year-olds at play. She trained to be a kindergarten teacher and had a head full of useful questions to ask the children to keep them on task. She had plenty of curriculum guides and felt that her job required her to fill the time quickly with the fewest possible distractions, and what gave her the feeling of being a success was the correct answer to a question she had asked. Then a high school science teacher called Bill asked to visit her class and what she noticed was that he used questions or made casual observations to which the children responded. She says:

'He and the children were constructing paper chains of ideas, factual and magical' and Bill supplied the glue'. (1991, p. 7)

But more was happening. Bill, she observed, was really interested in the children and in what they were doing and saying. Unlike Paley, he had no preconceptions about what children in the nursery should be doing. He was just plain curious about the way children solved problems.

This was the beginning of the changes to her teaching, but she still felt that she did not use what the children said and did. Although she heard them and saw them, she never used their ideas. The next step was to tape-record herself at work. One day she left the tape-recorder running after she left the play and when she later listened to the tape she found that what the children said in what she calls 'free play' was astounding and very different to what they said in her presence. She came to the startling conclusion that she was not needed to lead discussion. Instead she began to join in the play when appropriate and chart what she saw and heard. Over the year that followed she noticed that the initially simple dialogues of role play developed into long sequential dramas. She asked:

> 'How do the brief dialogues of the three-year-old so suddenly merge, at four, into long, sequential dramas that connect multitudes of events into a single plot? From a two-person up-and-down rhythm come choruses of intriguers who circumvent, outwit and disguise the unknown, the unwelcome and the unacceptable.' (1991, p. 14)

The class of 4-year-olds Paley followed over this year included Frederick who was deeply troubled by the birth of a baby. He brought his fear, his love, his anger, his uncertainty into the ongoing classroom dramas. Paley observed that whilst birthdays and bad guys are always the same in the children's imaginations, a baby is an uncertain symbol and changes from child to child, from class to class. Frederick and his peers had baby as super-hero and baby as whining and troublesome creature, and towards the end of the year the children invented baby Cringer and baby Cringer has a birth-day although no other babies do and doesn't have to change. According to Barney 'Babies can always stay a baby. And he has two fathers whenever he wants.' The rules are being made. Frederick asks if the baby needs brothers. Danger then appears and there is a shout to cover the baby because 'They're going to destroy the world.'

You have to read the book to fully enjoy the fantasy play revealed. When you become a playful practitioner, perhaps you will be able to witness something like this.

Bibliography

Abbott, L. and Nutbrown, C. (eds) (2001) *Experiencing Reggio Emilia*: *Implications for Pre-School Provision*. Buckingham, Philadelphia: Open University Press.

Abreu: www.ted.com/talks/jose_abreu_on_kids_transformed_by_music.html

Ager, L.P. (1980) Illustrated oral literature from southwestern Alaska. *Arts and Culture of the North IV(2)*: 225–227.

Allery, G. (1998) in S. Smidt (ed.) *The Early Years: A Reader*. London and New York: Routledge.

Athey, C. (1990) *Extending Thought in Young Children*: *A Parent-Teacher Partnership*. London: Paul Chapman Publishing.

Baghban, M. (1984) *Our Daughter Learns to Read and Write*: *A Case Study from Birth to Three*. International Reading Association.

Barbarin, O.A. and Richter, L.M. (2001) *Mandela's Children*: *Growing up in Post-Apartheid South Africa*. London and New York: Routledge.

Barrs, M. (1991) *Patterns of Learning*. Centre for Literacy in Primary Education.

Bateson, G. (1973) *Steps to an Ecology of Mind. Collected Essays on Anthropology, Psychology, Evolution and Epistemology*. St Albans: Paladin.

Bearne, E., Dombey, H. and Grainger, T. (eds) (2003) *Classroom Interactions in Literacy*. Maidenhead: Open University Press/McGraw-Hill.

Beetlestone, F. (1998) *Creative Children, Imaginative Teaching*. Buckingham, Philadelphia: Open University Press.

Bissex, G.L. (1980) *GNYS AT WRK: A Child Learns to Write and Read*. Cambridge, MA and London: Harvard University Press.

Blaise, M. (2005) *Playing It Straight*: *Uncovering Gender Discourses in the Early Childhood Classroom*. London and New York: Routledge.

Broadhead, P. (2004) *Early Years Play and Learning*: *Developing Social Skills and Cooperation*. London and New York: Routledge.

Brooker, L. (2009) "Just like having a best friend': How babies and toddlers construct relationships with their key workers in nurseries', in T. Papatheodorou and J. Moyles (eds), *Learning Together in the Early Years*: *Exploring Relational Pedagogy*. London and New York: Routledge.

Brostrom, S. (1997) 'Children's play: tools and symbols in frame play', in *Early Years*, 17(2): Spring.

Brown, B. (1998) *Unlearning Discrimination in the Early Years*. Stoke on Trent: Trentham Books.

Browne, N. (ed.) (1991) *Science and Technology in the Early Years*. Buckingham and Bristol: Open University Press.

Bruce, T. (1991) *Time to Play in Early Childhood Education*. London, Sydney and Auckland: Hodder & Stoughton.

Bruner, J. (1983) *Child's Talk*: *Learning to Use Language*. New York and Oxford: Oxford University Press.

Bruner, J. (1986) *Actual Minds, Possible Worlds*. Cambridge, MA and London: Harvard University Press.

Bruner, J. (1998) in G. Ceppi and M. Zini (eds) *Children, Spaces, Relations: Metaproject for an Environment for Young Children*. Reggio Emilia. Comune di Reggio Emilia.

Cannella, G.S. and Viruru, R. (2004) *Childhood and Postcolonization*: *Power, Education and Contemporary Practice*. London and New York: RoutledgeFalmer.

Canning, A. (2007) 'Children's empowerment in play', in *European Early Childhood Education Research Journal*, 15(2): 227–236.

Chamoiseau, P. (1993) *Childhood*. London: Granta.

Chomsky, N. (1980) *Rules and Representations*. Oxford: Blackwell.

deMarrais, K.B., Nelson, P.A. and Baker, J.H. (1994) 'Meaning in mud: Yup'ik Eskimo girls at play', in J.L. Roopnarine, J.E. Johnson and F.H. Hooper (eds), *Children's Play Diverse Cultures*. Albany: State University of New York Press.

Dunn, J. (1988) *The Beginnings of Social Understanding*. Oxford, UK and Cambridge, USA: Blackwell.

Dyson, A.H. (1997) *Writing Superheroes*: *Contemporary Childhood, Popular Culture, and Classroom Literacy*. New York: Teachers College Press.

Elkonin, D. (1980) *The Psychology of Play*. Madrid: Visor.

Elkonin, D. (1995) *Selected Works in Psychology*. Moscow: Pedagogika.

Faust, H. (1987) 'The multicultural curriculum in early childhood education', in G. Blenkin and A. Kelly (eds), *Early Childhood Education: Developmental curriculum*. Liverpool: Chapman.

Faust, H. (2010) 'Mathematical development in the Early Years Foundation Stage: problem-solving, reasoning and numeracy', in S. Smidt (ed.) (2010) *Key Issues in Early Years Education* (2nd edn). London and New York: Routledge.

Ferreiro, E. and Teberosky, A. (1979) *Literacy Before Schooling* (English edition 1982). Exeter, New Hampshire and London: Heinemann Education Books.

Freire, P. and Macedo, D. (eds) (1987) *Literacy*: *Reading the Word and the World*. London: Routledge and Kegan Paul.

Freud, A. and Burlingham, D. (1944) *Infants Without Families*: *The Case For and Against Residential Nurseries*. New York: International University Press.

Gopnik, A. (2009) *The Philosophical Baby*: *What Children's Minds Tell Us About Truth, Love and the Meaning of Life*. London: The Bodley Head.

Gopnik, A., Meltzoff, A.N. and Kuhl, P.K. (2001) *The Scientist in the Crib*: *What Early Learning Tells Us About the Mind*. New York: Harper Perennial.

Goouch, K. (2008) 'Understanding playful pedagogies, play narratives and play spaces', in *Early Years* 28(1), March 2008: 93–102.

Goouch, K. (2009) 'Forging and fostering relationships in play: whose zone is it anyway', in T. Papatheodorou and J. Moyles (eds), *Learning Together in the Early Years*: *Exploring Relational Pedagogy*. London and New York: Routledge.

Haylock, D. and Cockburn, A. (1989) *Understanding Early Years Mathematics*, pp. 2–4. Cited in Faust, H. (2010).

Holland, P. (2003) *We Don't Play with Guns Here: War, Weapon and Superhero Play in the Early Years*. Maidenhead, Philadelphia: Open University Press.

Hughes, A.M. (2009) *Problem Solving, Reasoning and Numeracy in the Early Years Foundation Stage*. London and New York: Routledge.

Hutt, S.J., Tyler, S., Hutt, C. and Christopherson, J.H. (1989) *Play, Exploration and Learning: A Natural History of Pre-School*. London and New York: Routledge.

ILEA Primary Guidelines (1986) *Science and Technology in the Early Years*. Cited in Browne (1991).

Isaacs, S. (1938) *Intellectual Growth in Young Children*. London: Routledge.

Karmiloff-Smith, A. (1992) *Beyond Modularity: A Developmental Perspective on Cognitive Science*. Cambridge, MA and London, UK: MIT Press.

Karmiloff-Smith, C. (1994) *Baby, It's You*. London: Ebury Press.

Kearney, C. (2003) *The Monkey's Mask: Identity, Memory, Narrative and Voice*. Stoke on Trent, UK and Sterling, USA.

Kingsolver, B. (1998) *The Bean Trees* (Virago edition 1990).

Kirk, J. (2008) 'The healing classrooms initiative and the Shimelba Refugee Camp, Ethiopia', in *Early Childhood Matters*, November 2008.

Kress, G. (1997) *Before Writing: Rethinking the Paths to Literacy*. London and New York: Routledge.

Kress, G. (1982) *Learning to Write* (second edition). London and New York: Routledge.

Lancy, D. (1977) 'The play behaviour of Kpelle children during rapid cultural change', in D.F. Lancy and B.A. Tindall (eds), *The Anthropological Study of Play: Problems and Prospects*. West Point. New York: Leisure Press.

Malaguzzi, L. (1984) *L'Occhio Se Salta Il Muro*. Giglio.

Marsh, J. and Hallett, J. (1999) *Desirable Literacies: Approaches to Language and Literacy in the Early Years*. London, Thousand Oaks, New Delhi: Paul Chapman Publishing.

Marsh, J. and Millard, E. (2000) *Literacy and Popular Culture: Using Children's Culture in the Classroom*. London, Thousand Oaks, New Delhi: Paul Chapman Publishing.

Martini, M. (1994) 'Peer Interactions in Polynesia: a view from the Marquesas', in J.L. Roopnarine, J.E. Johnson and F.H. Hooper (eds), *Children's Play Diverse Cultures*. Albany: State University of New York Press.

Meadows, S. (1993) *The Child as Thinker: The Development and Acquisition of Cognition in Childhood*. London and New York: Routledge.

Meek, M. (1991) *On Being Literate*. London: Bodley Head.

Mercer, N. (2000) *Words and Minds: How We Use Language to Think Together*. London: RoutledgeFalmer.

Moyles, J. (ed.) (2007) *Early Years Foundations: Meeting the Challenge*. Maidenhead: Open University Press.

Noschis, K. (1992) 'Child Development Theory and Planning for Neighborhood Play', in *Children's Environments*, 9(2): 3–9.

Orgocka, A. and Jones, I. (2007) 'Social inclusion and diversity through ECCE in northeastern Albania', in *Early Childhood Matters*, June 2007.

Paley, V.G. (1988) *Bad Guys Don't Have Birthdays: Fantasy Play at Four*. Chicago and London: The University of Chicago Press.

Paley, V.G. (1999) *The Kindness of Children*. Cambridge, MA and London, UK: Harvard University Press.

Papatheodorou, T. and Moyles, J. (eds) (2009) *Learning Together in the Early Years: Exploring Relational Pedagogy*. London and New York: Routledge.

Penn, H. (2005) *Unequal Childhoods: Young Children's Lives in Poor Countries*. London and New York: Routledge.

Penn, H. (ed.) (2000) *Early Childhood Services: Theory, Policy and Practice*. Buckingham, Philadephia: Open University Press.

Piaget, J. (1962) *Play, Dreams and Imitation in Childhood*. London: Routledge and Kegan Paul.

Rinaldi, C. (2006) *In Dialogue with Reggio Emilia: Listening, Researching and Learning*. London and New York: Routledge.

Robinson, T. (2009) www.ted.com/talks/lang/eng/ken_robinson_says_schools_kill_creativity.html

Rogoff, B. (1990) *Apprenticeship in Thinking*: Cognitive Development in Social Context. New York and Oxford: Oxford University Press.

Rogoff, B. and Lave, J. (eds) (1984, 1999) *Everyday Cognition*: Its Development in Social Context. Cambridge, MA and London, UK: Harvard University Press.

Rogoff, B., Mosier, C., Mistry, J. and Goncu, A. (1998) in M. Woodhead, D. Faulkner and K. Littleton (eds) *The Cultural Worlds of Early Childhood*. London and New York: Routledge in association with the Open University.

Roopnarine, J.L., Johnson, J.E. and Hooper, F.H. (eds) (1994) *Children's Play in Diverse Cultures*. Albany: State University of New York Press.

Roskos, K.A. and Christie, J.F. (2000) *Play and Literacy in Early Childhood*: Research From Multiple Perspectives. Mahwah, NJ and London: Lawrence Erlbaum Associates.

Roy, A. (1997) *The God of Small Things*. New York: Flamingo.

Sayeed, Z. and Guerin, E. (2000) *Early Years Play*: A Happy Medium for Assessment and Intervention. London: David Fulton.

Schiller, F. 'Über die ästhetische Erziehung des Menschen in einer Reihe von Brienfen' (1793/94), in: *Schillers Werke*, Band 5, Leipzig O. J.

Smidt, S. (1988) 'Making links: children talking about reality'. *English in Education*: Oracy Edition Spring 1988 22(1): NATE.

Smidt, S. (ed.) (1998) *The Early Years: A Reader*. London and New York: Routledge.

Smidt, S. (2006) *The Developing Child in the 21st Century: A Global Perspective on Child Development*. London and New York: Routledge.

Smidt, S. (2009) *Introducing Vygotsky: A Guide for Practitioners and Students in the Early Years*. London and New York: Routledge.

Smith, F. (1978) *Reading*. Cambridge and London: Cambridge University Press.

Smith, F. (1982) *Writing and the Writer*. New York: Holt, Rinehart and Winston,

Strandell, H. (2000) 'What is the use of children's play?' In H. Penn (ed.), *Early Childhood Services*: Theory, Policy and Practice. Buckingham, Philadephia: Open University Press.

Stern, D. (1985 1st edn)/1998 (2nd edn) *The Interpersonal World of the Infant: A View from Psychoanalysis and Developmental Psychology*. New York: Basic Books.

Trevarthen, C. (1998) (original 1995) 'The child's need to learn a culture', in M. Woodhead, D. Faulkner and K.I. Littleton (eds), *The Cultural Worlds of Early Childhood*. London and New York: Routledge.

Vecchi, V. (1993) 'The role of the Atelierista', in C. Edwards, L. Gandini and G. Forman (eds), *The Hundred Languages of Children*. Norwood, NJ: ablex.

Vecchi, V. (2009) *Art and Creativity in Reggio Emilia* (Contesting Early Childhood). London and New York: Routledge.

Vygotsky, L.S. (1962) *Thought and Language*. Cambridge: MIT Press.

Vygotsky, L.S. (1967) 'Play and its role in the mental development of the child', *Soviet Psychology* 5: 6–18.

Vygotsky, L.S. (1978) *Mind in Society: Development of Higher Psychological Processes*. Cambridge, MA: Harvard University Press.

Vygotsky, L.S. (1981) 'The genesis of higher mental functions', in J.V. Wertsch (ed.), *The Concept of Activity in Soviet Psychology*. Armonk, NY: Sharpe.

Whitehead, M. (1990 1st edn; 1997 2nd edn; 2004 3rd edn) *Language and Literacy in the Early Years*. London: SAGE.

Whitehead, M. (1997) *Language and Literacy in the Early Years*. London: Paul Chapman Publishers.

Woodhead, M., Faulkner, D. and Littleton, K. (eds) (1998) *The Cultural Worlds of Early Childhood*. London and New York: Routledge.

Worthington, M. and Carruthers, E. (2003) *Children's Mathematics: Making Marks, Making Meaning*. London: PCP.

Index

Lightning Source UK Ltd.
Milton Keynes UK
UKOW06f0014101015

260240UK00004B/61/P

9 780415 558822